CHAPTE

Dedication

I want to thank my husband Jason, my mom, and dad for enveloping me with endless love and support on this long trek, which has made me the strong, confident woman I am today. I have been able to travel on this journey and finally unlock doors that have been closed for so long. Thank you. Jason, thank you for being my rock and my voice of reason, even though at times I did not listen. I also want to thank my two boys Dominic and Nicolas Tillou, who have made me realize how wonderful motherhood is, and how truly blessed I am. You boys are my moon, sun and stars.

Acknowledgments

I owe a huge thank you to my true angels, Elaine and Diana, my ALMA friend Candy, fellow New Jersey women Darlene and Dotty, fellow adoptees Stacey and Ann, and my best friends Melissa, Carol and Stacey. A gracious thank you to Dr. Eugene Merecki for believing in me and my quirks, and leading me on the path to my diagnosis. Thank you to Dr. Natasha Shur, the pediatric geneticist who has given me the reason for my "quirks." Thank you to each and every one of you for making this journey and this book possible.

Prologue

An Adoptee's Perspective: Written in January, 2013

The day is January 12, 1980. The hospital I assume is Valley Hospital in Ridgewood New Jersey. The time is 1:06 am. A baby girl is brought into the world. Her mother may have held her briefly, felt her little body against herself for a moment's time. She may not have. Her mother may have decided not to hold her daughter at all, and had a nurse immediately take her because the pain was too great. Only her mother and the nurses know what happened that morning.

The baby was taken into a foster home in Ridgewood, New Jersey and stayed there for one month. On February 9, 1980 in Ellicott City, Maryland, the Kulak family received a phone call from an adoption agency. There was a baby girl waiting to become part of a family and showered with love. On February 14, 1980, commonly

5

known as Valentine's Day, that baby girl became part of the Kulak family. That baby girl was me.

At the age of 4, I gained an understanding that my adoptive mom Debbie Kulak did not give birth to me, but the Kulak's were still my family. The middle school years were when I began to question who I was, and who my birth parents were. I didn't spend a lot of time thinking about being adopted, but certain events triggered questions. My birthday and Valentine's Day were two days that I was very thankful for my family, but hints of wonder and sadness would enter my mind. I would wonder, "Does my birth mom think of me on these days? What is she doing now? Why did she give me away? If I weren't adopted, how would my life be different? "

As major events have happened in my life, these questions have been in the forefront and have become more prominent as I have gotten older. At my school graduations and at my wedding, I couldn't help but wonder what my birth mom would think.

I have had conversations with people that don't understand why these thoughts are so prevalent in my mind since I was adopted at such a young age. No matter what age you are adopted, the facts remain the same: Your birth mother made a choice to give you up. You may know why, you may not. If you don't know, you may wonder your whole life. In some cases, as in mine, you don't know your medical history, who your biological family is, or where you got your physical traits from. I feel like a puzzle with pieces missing.

My two young sons are the only two genetic ties I have ever identified with. One day, maybe I will discover genetic ties to my birth family. Until that day, I will be thankful for the wonderful family I was adopted into, and the selfless choice my birth mom made in the early hours of January 12, 1980.

*****

Well, I finally got to meet her. On June 7, 2013 at 8:30 am,
I walked outside and the clammy, misty air enveloped me.
I drove down the road, and parked in the tiny parking lot of
our village post office. She was waiting for me. I opened
the front passenger door to my car, and helped her in. I
drove like a turtle down the roads toward my house in the
little town of Voorheesville, New York. I pulled into my
driveway, and turned the car off, my right hand catching
my eye as it trembled. I stepped out of my car, holding
myself steady with my left hand as my legs started to
buckle under me. I steadied myself, and caught my breath.
I walked around the front of the car and opened her door. I
helped her out, and took her inside, making sure she didn't
fall. Chester, our German shepherd came to sniff her out.
Deciding she was ok to be in the house, he retreated back to
the couch. I texted my husband, and told him she had

8

arrived. He asked me if I was ok. I texted back that I was,

that I just felt weird. I sat her down and spoke to her. She

just sat there, stoic. I went into the guest room and turned

on a song for us to listen to. I came back and placed my

hand on her. I cried, teardrops falling onto the top of her.

When the song ended, I stopped, wiped my tears away, and

left the room. It was a bitter sweet moment.

Chapter One

A Daughter to Be

In the early morning hours of January 12, 1980, a baby girl entered this world. Tears of confusion, fear and sorrow fell from the woman's eyes as she listened to her baby's first cry. Her hands lightly held that baby girl, knowing if she held on any tighter, the decision would be that much harder.

On February 9, 1980, a phone call came through to a couple who had also shed many tears of sorrow. This couple had been on a journey of sadness for two years, and they were ready for a change. February 13, 1980, a mother, father, and their four year old son embarked on a trip to meet a little baby who would dry their tears.

I came into the Kulak's life a couple years after their daughter Loren passed away. She was only five days old and passed away due to complications of being a preemie. The Kulak's were devastated after Loren's passing, but God had great plans for the Kulaks, and for me. After the passing of their daughter, my parents turned to their Presbyterian Church for support. A few of the church members discussed the idea of adoption with them. They told my parents about a Christian adoption agency in New Jersey. This adoption agency would come into my parents' lives at the right time, and years later would play a vital role in my adult life.

In April of 1979, my parents decided to talk to the adoption agency about their eligibility requirements to be adoptive parents. They felt they wanted another child, and thought it may help in healing their wounded hearts. They went through the application process, and were contacted for their first interview in July of 1979. Their second interview was in October of 1979, and on February 1, 1980 my parents were approved for a child to be a part of their family. My parents were happy they had been approved, and went on with their daily activities, caring for their son and each other, not expecting to receive a proposal about a week later.

On February 9, 1980, a social worker from the adoption agency called my parents. She described a baby girl who had been born on January 12, 1980 and given over to their agency. My parents became intoxicated with excitement and nerves. They inquired about my birth mother. My adoption was a closed one, which meant my parents were allowed basic ethnic, health, educational, and marital information on my birth mother. They were told there was nothing significant in my health history, yet my parents were skeptical. How could they trust a woman they never met, a woman who didn't or couldn't raise her own daughter? Who knew if what they were told about me and my birth mother was fact or fiction? My parents were advised my birth mother claimed she did not know she was pregnant, smoked a pack of cigarettes a day, drank throughout her pregnancy, and she may have been intoxicated during the delivery. My parents were also assured in writing she was not an alcoholic. My parents tried to believe what was told to them, but there was this doubt that kept creeping in. The unknown was not a comfortable place.

My parents simultaneously felt happiness and fear. They thanked the social worker for the information. They were then invited to come to New Jersey to meet me and make a decision to either take me home or let me remain up for adoption. They packed up a suitcase and with my 4 year old brother in tow, headed to North Haledon, New Jersey. They arrived at a Howard Johnson Inn, and then trekked over to the agency. Awaiting them on February 13, 1980 was this little sweet pea. They sat down on a plaid couch and I was placed into my mom's arms. They stayed for a while, smiling, crying, and watching this little girl sleep.

After a while, my parents and brother handed me back to the social worker, and were told to go back to the hotel and think about their decision. The loss of Loren had created immense holes in their hearts. Their minds were filled with joy at the chance to have a daughter, but also filled with doubt. I had no prenatal care, and although the adoption agency's pediatrician had considered me healthy, there were so many unknowns. My father expressed that he wanted to take the chance. He believed God was working in their lives, and I was meant to be their daughter.

My mom believed I was born to become a part of a family, but wasn't sure it was their family. She was filled with worry about my health. She did not want to lose another daughter. On Valentine's Day in 1980, after much discussion, tears, embraces and prayer, my parents and brother went back to the agency, and headed back home as a family of four.

Chapter Two

Childhood Memories

I remember every Valentine's Day as a child. It was a special day for my whole family. My parents would get a cake to commemorate my Adoption Day. They were always cognizant that my adoption was a life altering moment for all parties involved. I gave them a daughter and their son a sister, someone to admire and idolize him. They gave me life and love.

My birthdays were always fun filled with games, friends, family and laughter. I have always loved celebrating my birthday. As a young child I enjoyed it because I got the opportunity to have my favorite homemade pasta dinner, play games with friends, eat lots of cake, and of course open tons of presents. As I got older, I realized how ironic my birthday actually is. Most people that are not adopted celebrate their birthday with those who were present at their birth. They have those *same* relatives who tell the *same* birth story every year, "I remember the day you were born…" My family was not there for my birth. My parents know my birth mom was almost forty years old, she may have been intoxicated, and I appeared to be full term. On the flip side, it is indeed a wonderful day to celebrate, because my birth led to me becoming a Kulak.

Kindergarten through my senior year in high school were years of making and breaking friendships and entering the dating world. They were filled with laughter, tears and accomplishments. They were years interspersed with feelings, fears and decisions.

Elementary school was a time of firsts. I learned I was left handed, I learned I loved to write descriptive stories and poetry, and I gained an understanding of what being adopted meant. My parents never sat me down on a specific day and told me where I came from. From the

17

moment they took me home, they started reading me children's books on adoption. They never hid my adoption story from anyone, especially me. As I got older, they continued to read adoption books to me, and they would answer any questions I had. My parents believed that an adoptee should know where they came from early on. There are different views on when to tell an adoptee they are adopted, if they are told at all, and there are not right or wrong times. It depends on the family dynamic and beliefs. As I got older, they told me about their daughter Loren and how she got sick and went up to be with God, and after a couple years they decided they wanted another child to love. I understood their explanation, and I knew I was loved tremendously and unconditionally. I didn't have any reservations about being a Kulak. I was a happy, well-adjusted child.

My parents created a baby book for me, and I remember my mom taking it out for me to see when I was around seven years old. My mom sat next to me as we went through every page. There were photos of the baby shower my mom's friends threw for her after I came home. There were photos of my first and second birthdays, and my mom had written on every page. This book was full of love and happy memories. In the back of the book, there was a little folder to put mementos. I pulled out everything in this folder, and I found a card I had made for my parents. I must have been four or five based on the drawing. Then again, my art skills have not improved at all, so I could've drawn it in my twenties. It was a photo of two babies in separate cribs in a big room, and two people outside double doors. They were smiling, and the babies in the cribs were crying. Above the picture I had written, "*Mom Dad I Love you very much. And Im Happy that you culde adoped me. And that you Love me very much. And I Love All of You. The End.*" That card stated my sentiments about adoption, both at a young age and as an adult.

It was in elementary school that I realized the differences between my family and me. Elementary school is when I found I was left handed and nobody else in my family was. My friends and family would hold their hands up to mine, and admire how long and spindle like my fingers were. My family's fingers were average. My feet were nicknamed banana peels because they were absurdly narrow. My mom loved shoe shopping, but not for me. Although these physical traits were the opposite of my family's traits, I didn't see them in a negative light. In my mind, these traits made me special.

People in my classes in elementary school never looked at me as, "the adopted one." Some didn't know, and others knew and it didn't matter. I had a classmate in second grade who called me a liar when I stated I was adopted. I remember feeling hurt and angry. The next day I brought in my birth certificate as proof that I was indeed a child of adoption. My classmate never questioned me again. Thinking back, I do not know how showing my birth certificate proved anything. At 8 years old, a birth certificate was a birth certificate, amended or not. My classmate had no idea what she was supposed to be looking at that was different from her birth certificate.

In third grade I made best friends with a girl named Anna. She invited me to spend the night on a Friday night after school. I was so excited, and I kept writing her notes throughout the week asking her if she still wanted to have the sleepover. I wanted so much to be with her at her house Friday night, because in my eyes it would mean she accepted me as a friend. She was patient with me, as patient as a third grade girl can be, and the sleepover happened. This situation was me needing acceptance by others. My insecurities may be able to be traced to thoughts about why my birth mom gave me away. Did she not accept me as I was, an innocent child brought into this world by her? Maybe subconsciously I always thought if my birth mom gave me up, that meant she didn't accept me for who I was. Maybe this thought transcended into my thoughts regarding friendships, and I always worried that my friends would not accept me and cast me aside, just like I felt my birth mom did. I do not remember these questions permeating my mind throughout my childhood, but my actions point to feelings of not being accepted as a possible player in the game of emotions. Years later, a diagnosis would reveal the reason for my incessant note writing to my friend. It had nothing to do with my inner turmoil, but everything to do with the way my brain had been formed at birth.

Throughout my elementary school years, I was a very conscientious worker, as the teachers wrote on my report card each year. I strived to please the teachers, I wanted them to be proud of Rebecca Kulak. My yearning to please adults transcended across classrooms and into my home. I wanted my parents to be proud of their daughter. I never wanted to be a disappointment. I remember always putting my plates in the dish washer, washing the coffee pot, sweeping the foyer floor, and then going to tell my parents what I had accomplished. I craved that praise. My mom signed me up for Girl Scouts when I was four. I disliked it, but I didn't want to upset her, so I stayed in it. My mom would take me shopping for clothes, and I never voiced a negative opinion. I would tell her I liked everything she bought. This need to please my parents carried over into adulthood. It appeared throughout my marriage, and affected the relationship between my husband and me. When I married my husband, we became one. Decisions were supposed to be made between us, and if others disagreed, that is the way it would be. There would be discussions about child rearing, my husband would have a certain opinion, and I would agree with him initially. Then, I would talk to my parents, they would give suggestions, and I would automatically bounce over to their side, because I did not want to go against them. Years later, I wondered if there was a link between being adopted and craving praise from those that adopted me. The Primal Wound by Nancy Verrier (1993) states those that are adopted feel sadness when they are taken from their birth mothers, because that innate bond is torn. In the depths of my mind, did I maybe think the bond between my adoptive parents and I could also be broken? Is that why I tried to please them all the time? This reasoning made perfect sense in my mind, until I received an eye opening diagnosis at age 34, and learned one of the characteristics is immaturity (www.nofas.org, 2014), I believe my disorder is the sole reason for my actions. I acted like a child who desired approval of their parents first and foremost. I was, and still am, a grown up with a child's mind.

I have been seeing a counselor for about 5 years now. He has helped me see the error of my ways when it comes to marriage, and I am working on being ok with my parents and me not always agreeing. It is a part of growing up and learning to be part of a couple. It is about letting go of parts of the past, and learning that my parents have unconditional love towards me. If J and I choose a different path than my parents would choose, it is ok, they will still love me. It is a hard lesson to learn, especially when I am dealing with the mindset of a younger persona.

My parents were always cognizant of the ages when I may start to question my adoption and my identity. When I was in fifth grade, my parents signed me up for a month long class at my school with an adoption counselor. There were about five of us, ranging from third to fifth grade. It was beneficial to be able to speak out about what being adopted meant to me, amongst peers my age, and to realize I was not alone in my thoughts. In fifth grade, I defined adoption as my birth mom not being able to take care of me for whatever reason, and my parents adopting me into their family. My feelings were still superficial at ten years old.

That would soon change as my pre-teen and teenage years
crept into the pathways of my life.

Chapter Three

Confusion

As I entered my teenage years, I noticed myself becoming confused about what peer group I fit into. I tried every group, hoping to find my niche. I went from the geeks to the popular girls to the jocks. I felt like I didn't belong anywhere. I had no problem being friendly with people, and I was comfortable with Carol and Melissa, two of my closest friends, but that was where my comfort zone ended. I attributed it to being a teenager, and just assumed most teenagers were going through the same awkward stage. We were taught in seventh grade health class that our teenage years would be full of hormones and figuring out who we would become as an adult. When I was thirty years old, and still felt like I didn't fit into a social group, I wondered, "Is it possibly due to being adopted, and not knowing where I come from?" If I didn't know where I came from, wouldn't it be difficult to know what type of social groups to immerse myself into? This reasoning makes sense, but in actuality, a different reason surfaced in my mid-thirties and answered why I was unable to find a group I fit into. I was emotionally on a younger level (www.nofas.org, 2013).

In sixth grade, my family was planning a trip to Kings Dominion, an amusement park in Virginia. My parents gave me permission to take two friends. I recall I was in gym class, and I decided to ask a girl I had just become friendly with a couple weeks prior to come with me to the park. She was very sweet and told me she would ask her parents. I think secretly she was taken aback that we had just become acquaintances, not even quite friends, and I was asking her to go on a family day trip. She ended up declining the invitation, just saying she was unable to attend. No reason behind it. I will never know if it is because I pressed too hard and too fast for a friendship with her. I found myself in similar situations after this. I would have a friendly conversation with a classmate for the first time, and then invite them over for a sleep over the next day. We barely knew one another. I think back over my actions, and I wouldn't consider myself pushy, but rather needy, impulsive, a younger version of myself. I took every simple, nice gesture from people as them wanting to be my best friend. I was seeking acceptance with everyone.

 I did originally believe these instances were because I wanted to ease that feeling of rejection that lurked right under the surface of my mind, that feeling that I believe was implanted the day I was given up by my birth mom (Verrier, 2003). I now know my overzealous and forward nature is because of a choice my birth mother made while pregnant. Being friendly with everyone, including strangers and those we have just met, is a common characteristic of those who are products of the same choice my birth mom made when she was pregnant (http://come-over.to/FAS/PDF/SoftSigns.pdf, 2001, 2002). We may think we are being social, but in reality it is not a normal social practice, and can come across as needy and creepy.

I have taken a look back over my later teenage years, and there is a definite pattern of wanting to please people and gain their attention and adoration, even at the expense of those I love. I had a pattern of seeking attention from older men twice my age or more. Men I barely knew. I remember playing basketball outside in my driveway when I was about 13 years old. I remember talking to myself, which I have always done. I remember talking loudly though, explaining my every move to shoot the ball. I would keep looking at my next door neighbor out in his driveway, washing his car. He was about 10 years younger than my parents. I wanted him to look up. I wanted his attention. Some may say it was my age that made me seek attention. For other 13 year olds, that may have been the reason. Years later I would understand that for me, my actions had to do with my inability to understand appropriate relationships.

When I became a freshman in high school, I started running Cross Country. I befriended our assistant coach, who was also a substitute teacher in my school. He became friends with *all* the girls. He was very immature for being 30. I thrived on the attention he gave. He would give me tips on running, and sometimes he would run with the girl's team. Over the next couple years, our acquaintance deepened. In my junior year, I decided to take the reins of the relationship. I invited the whole team to Pizza Hut after a cross country meet, including our assistant coach. Everyone bailed, except this coach. I was elated to have his attention all to myself. Over the next couple years, our relationship grew into a flirty friendship, complete with flirty notes stuck inside my locker and glimpses through my classroom door when he was substituting. I felt such a rush. I did not see anything wrong with the fact he was a teacher, a coach, or twice my age. Our relationship escalated into being a couple. I kept it hidden from my parents until the principal came and escorted me out of English class my senior year. He walked me into his office, and there stood a social worker and a police officer. My secret was out. To this day I do not know who suspected, but I am glad they did and I am glad they turned me in. If nothing had been said, there is no telling where my life would have led. I went home that day and called my parents on the phone. I told them over the receiver what I had been doing, and my mom had someone drive her home because she was too upset to drive. My father and mother sat me down at the kitchen table, and they asked that I explain the past few months of lies and deceit. I explained the relationship, and how I loved him, and how age didn't matter. They looked at me, appalled. For the next year, I would break up and reunite with this man, and sneak around multiple times. I would go off to college dating him, and eventually break it off for good.

In the fall of 1998, I attended The State University of Geneseo in Western New York for college. Early in the second semester of my freshman year, I had a couple girlfriends take me aside and tell me I looked so unhappy and so lost. I laid in bed that night thinking about those words. The next morning, I looked in the mirror. I didn't recognize the girl staring back. Dark circles shadowed my eyes, stringy hair framed my face, and oversized sweatshirts and sweatpants embodied me. The ensemble was completed with Tevas and running socks. In that moment I decided I needed to make a change. I had been getting to know a Christian group at my college for the past few months, and with their strength and courage that they poured into my heart, on February 11, 1999, I called up the track coach, and broke it off. I have not spoken to him since that day. February 11th, 1999 would be the date of another major event, only I wouldn't be made aware of it until years later.

The entire time we were together, about 15 months, I kept saying age didn't matter. I kept saying there was nothing wrong with our relationship. It took dating guys my age, growing up, getting married, and having my own children to realize how wrong that relationship was. The social worker and police officer who pulled me out of class referred to me as the *victim.* As did every other adult I came into contact with. I used to say I was not the victim, I understood what was going on, and I was a consenting adult. Well, years later, I realized I *was* the victim. I may have been 15 when the friendship started, and 18 when we became intimate, but my mental age was years less. 5-7 years younger I would say. I was mentally 8 years old when the friendship started. My brain saw this guy as an adult who knew right from wrong. If he thought it was ok, then it was. I was mentally about 11 years old when we became intimate. My mental age still considered him an adult, and I looked to him for guidance and right from wrong. I believed he knew what was right for me, and for us.

Now, I always received constant attention and praise from family and friends, there was absolutely no need to seek it elsewhere. It was an insatiable need to feel wanted, and that need would be fulfilled momentarily, and then I would need to search again. While a piece of this internal wanting may have had to do with my birth mom separating from me at birth, a majority of it is because of the damage done to me when in the womb. It is the impulsivity and the naïve, trusting nature that characterizes the brain damage (http://come-over.to/FAS/PDF/SoftSigns.pdf, 2001, 2002). It intrigues me, and disgusts me at the same time, that one decision my birth mom made had the ability to, and did affect *my* ability to make appropriate decisions.

When I started college, I was hopeful that I would find my place in college, like I had with my running group in high school. I had heard from my friend's siblings that college was wonderful and it was a time to find oneself. I was all about that. Unfortunately my college experience was not filled with finding myself and a new set of friends. Throughout college I sometimes felt awkward with the people I lived with. I tried to fit in, I tried to be comfortable, but I just wasn't. I remember at times feeling like I forced myself to laugh and smile when everyone else was. I was a chameleon, blending into my surroundings, yet I felt like a storm cloud in a clear blue sky. I tried to understand why I felt this way. I remember the girls in my dorm suite would all be laughing and joking. I would try to say something funny, and it wouldn't receive the same laughter. I felt like the new girl at times, even when I was in my last year. Well, now I know why. There is that saying, if only I knew then what I know now. If only I knew my brain was constantly in a struggle. Sometimes if a person's brain is different than the average person's brain, she can have difficulty connecting in social groups, because she isn't at the same intellectual or emotional level (www.nofas.org, 2013). That was me.

My college years were full of learning about the art of studying, becoming a Speech Pathologist, and partying. I remember in the summer after my freshman year in college, I attended a party with my best friend's boyfriend. I met a guy there who was clearly intoxicated. He excused himself at one point, and I continued to have a conversation with my best friend's boyfriend. After about twenty minutes, I became aware that the "guy" had not come back. I decided I would call it a night, and slipped through the front door. I started walking towards my car, and noticed the "guy" laying on the grass. He said he was staring at the stars. I sat down next to him and he sat up. He shivered as a cool summer breeze swept through. He stood up and stumbled next to me as I made it to my car. I told him to get in my car and warm up. He fell into my vehicle, and we started making out. He kept passing out on me, so I told him I had to get home. I walked to the passenger side of my vehicle and opened the passenger door. I held onto his arm as he stepped out of my car. As I drove away, I looked over my shoulder and could see the outline of a guy passed out on the front lawn. The "guy" and I had exchanged numbers, and I waited to hear from him the next day. It took all the restraint I had to not pick up the phone and call him. I waited until two days after we met, and then I picked up the receiver. I called his number three times that day, the first time I left a message, the second time I got his parents on the phone who told me he was "busy" and the third time he answered. We set up a movie date for that night. It ended up not being a date at all. We pulled into the parking lot of the theater, talked for about ten minutes, and I remember I was trying to get him to kiss me. He was not into it. He clearly did not want to be there with me, and was not attracted to a stalker. He drove me home and that was that. As I reflect back on these moments, I realize I was a guy's worst nightmare. I was a cling on. I was 19, acting like a 12 year old girl who wanted a guy to pay attention to her, at any cost. I did not want to be rejected. I stalked this poor man until he agreed to meet me, just to appease me. I am one of those people that fear being rejected with the most simplest of daily tasks, such as when I send an email, text message or make a phone call, and the recipient does not respond within one day. I have been this way as long as I can remember, and I did think being an adoptee who witnessed rejection at birth may have played a role in my feelings that have followed me through to the present. Although I was almost 20 when I went on that date, I became a nervous 13-16 year old who wanted everyone to like them. I wanted to be popular, I didn't want to be ignored. In my thirties, I had a breakthrough. The breakthrough was discovering my birth

mom's selfish decision during pregnancy was the reason

for those feelings of rejection.

Chapter Four

Who?

"I was searching for my past…for a mirror to my being…"

It was in my junior year of high school when I took notice of the black file cabinet in my parents' computer room downstairs. Now, I had always been a curious individual. There was a drawer with "MISC" Written on the front. I came home from school one day and tiptoed downstairs, even though nobody was home. I think I was hoping if I tiptoed my conscience would not see what I was doing. I opened the file cabinet, and started pushing the hanging files forward. I came to a file marked, "Adoption." I unhooked it and pulled it out. I made sure to keep a space between the folders where I took it from, so I could put it back with nobody noticing it had been tampered with. I sat on the floor with my legs crossed, and placed the folder in my lap. I opened it and sifted through it. I found a sheet of *non-identifying information* typed up by the adoption agency, and court documents typed by legal representatives explaining different court dates my parents had to attend for my adoption proceedings. Since it was a closed adoption, my birth mom was not at any of the court proceedings, and my birth father was apparently never aware he had a child per the documents I found. I found a document that the social worker had drafted up for my parents in preparation of meeting me. Since they were not there for the first month of my birth, they were not aware of my routine. This document introduced me and my routines. I smiled when I looked at it. It was written as if it came from me as a newborn. That was pretty much the extent of the file, besides directions to the agency. I carefully kept the papers in order, and placed them back in the file. I returned the file, and closed the drawer. A couple days later, I crept downstairs after school again, and I pulled the file. I placed it in my backpack and that night I went to the library. I made copies of the file's contents. I remember my nerves as I watched the copies being made. I kept envisioning my father going into that filing cabinet and noticing the file had gone missing. I grabbed the copies from the copier, stuck them back in the folder, put the folder into my back pack, and drove home. The next day after school I returned the folder to its home. I was never questioned by my father. The copies I had made I placed in a folder in my desk. I had no plans for them at that time. I just wanted them because they were a written scroll of my past. It wasn't much, but it was something.

Before my sons were born, I looked in a mirror every day and saw me. That was it. I didn't see a resemblance to anyone, because I didn't know anybody biologically tied to me. My desire to "search til I find" for my birth mom Joan was ignited a few months after having my second son, Nicolas. Every moment I rocked him to sleep, the same question burned within my soul. "Did Joan ever hold me after I was born?" This question would be the start of many questions that would line the journey into my past. I looked at Nicolas, and saw that he had my eye shape, my ears, and my husband's nose and face shape. I felt this genetic bond between him and myself. I desired to have that between my biological mother and me. If she and I reunited, would that genetic bond that was severed at birth be tied back together? Even if it wasn't, I still wanted to be able to look across a table and see a woman who held me within for nine months before making the selfless decision she did.

When I held Nicolas as a newborn, I couldn't wrap my head around how someone could give up their own child. Listening to my child cry, picking him up, and knowing he sensed his mom and stopped crying because he knew I was his mom…there isn't another feeling like it. I talk about this moment because I am sure there are some adoptees out there that search here and there, but in their minds say they don't understand how anyone could become obsessed with searching for people they have never met. I didn't think I would become obsessed. I thought I would go through life as I always had, writing poetry about adoption around my birthday and my birth mom's birthday, searching on the computer here and there for brief moments, but never go to the extent I did to find my roots. It took a specific life changing event for me to make a decision that I would search until I found. Not every adoptee will have an event that turns a switch inside them, and shuts them out from the rest of the world while they find their missing puzzle pieces. Life can take unexpected twists and turns, as can searching for your past.

I would sit feeding or rocking Nicolas and wonder why I didn't feel the desire to search after I had my first son, Dominic. I do remember after giving birth to Dominic, I recognized his cry from down the hall, amongst the other babies. I remember him being placed in my arms for the first time, six hours after he was born, and him quieting down immediately. I remember during those moments feeling an intense love, and being in awe at this incredible creation. I remember wondering how a mother could give up her child after seeing her and holding her for the first time. That is as far as my desire to know went. I think because I was so immersed in trying to figure out the parameters of being a first time mom, I didn't have any room to wonder and search. I also was a 28 year old with a 18-20 year old mind, a mind that really didn't understand how to take care of a newborn. I had a mind that was very easily overwhelmed, due to being saturated in a toxic substance while in utero. I think 4 years later when Nicolas was born, since I was more comfortable being a mom, I was able to let more intimate feelings about my birth mom Joan creep into my mind.

I started searching for Joan around May of 2012. I wanted to know my roots, I wanted to meet her and finally see my reflection.　I had my "non-identifying information" given to my parents by the adoption agency the day they took me home.　I had her date of birth, first name, ethnicity, her hobbies and occupation.　This information wasn't detailed or extensive, but Joan's first name, her date of birth and her ethnicity would be the three keys that would unlock her identity.

REBECCA LEIGH KULAK

BORN: Jan. 12, 1980 at 1:06 AM at Ridgewood, New Jersey

6 lb., 14 oz.; 19" long

VDRL negative

RH A positive

APGAR: 8 @ 1 min.
9 @ 5 min.

PKU test done 1/17/80 no notification - OK

40-week pregnancy; spontaneous vaginal delivery w/ saddle block

1/18/80 - 6 lb., 12 oz. - discharged to Bethany Christian Services,
considered "very healthy"

1/30/80 - 7lb., 5oz. - (21"?) - seen by BCS pediatrician

Mother

Born 8/11/40; unmarried.

Tall, thin - 5' 10", 160 lb.; Brown hair and eyes, fair complexion

Polish descent; Catholic

High school graduate; barmaid

Enjoys swimming, horseback riding

No information given on maternal grandparents

Nothing significant in health history

Quiet person, was under some stress in the hospital

Claims she didn't know she was pregnant; no pre-natal care; smokes;
may have been some drinking during pregnancy - not an alcoholic

Didn't feel in a position to raise a child

Father

Last name and address unknown (3 dates)

6' 1", 200 lb.; Brown hair and eyes, medium complexion

Irish descent

No medical history

Interested in boating, sailing

Mother signed release and waiver of court hearing on 1/17/80. No
release signed by putative father. BCS will write affidavit
that father was unknown and could not be reached.

My non-identifying information

When I first decided to search, I told my husband my desire, and he told me he understood to the extent he could. Never having gone through it himself, he said he would be there for me. I quickly became engrossed, obsessed if you will, about searching for Joan. I have always had an obsessive nature, as was seen with the scenario that played out with that poor soul I stalked by phone. I realized a couple years later that my obsessive nature was due to a few short circuits in my brain. An obsessive nature can be debilitating to a person and their friendship and family circles, and mine did pull me away from my family. As much as I wish I did not become as obsessed with searching as I did, I also know it was my obsessive nature that got me to where I ended up.

Now, I have had a plethora of conversations with people asking me, "What about your birth father?" When I first became interested in knowing who my birth mom was, my birth father was like a fart in the wind: there for a second, and then gone. It appears, in my encounters with other adoptees, that this is often the case. Adoptees have an unseen bond with their birth moms, just like every mom and child. Nobody can see it, but everyone involved can feel it. Like magnets attracting one another, mother and child feel a pull when they see each other for the first time—whether that meeting is when a child is born, or when a child finds his or her biological mother. In the midst of searching for Joan, when I was hitting wall after wall, I decided to search for my birth father. I would type my birth father's first name into a search engine, and then write, "New Jersey Sailing." My non-identifying sheet of information stated he liked boating and sailing. It also stated he was Irish. So, I would also peruse sailors with Irish last names. I reached out to a handful and only heard back from two. One man was sweet in his response, wishing me luck in my endeavors. The other man wrote me back a one liner with two words, extremely vulgar. I thought maybe because he was an extremely wealthy boater maybe he was nervous I was after his fortune. I debated about responding to his email. I decided I would, and I just wrote that I couldn't care less about his fame and fortune. I just wanted to

know my biological father and find my roots. Of course, he

never responded, and after that experience, I put my, "Who's

Your Daddy" question up on a shelf.

Chapter Five

Obsessed Much?

One of the first steps I took when I began searching for my birth mom was I began to network with the adoption agency I was adopted through. I made a phone call, and was placed in touch with a social worker who would become my go to person throughout my searching journey. There became an ongoing dialogue between this social worker and myself. I found she understood my innate desire to know more, as she was an adoptive mom and understood the frustration of the New Jersey adoption record system. As a social worker for a New Jersey adoption agency, she was bound by New Jersey adoption laws. Closed adoptions in New Jersey have sealed records, until January 1, 2017. The only way to get those records opened before January 1, 2017 is by a court order. This law of opening records in 2017 was passed after my journey had ended. I think it bothered the social worker as much as me that in her possession right in front of her she had my birth mom's full name, and she could not disclose it. Throughout the stent of my search, I would email the social worker questions, hopeful for answers. One of the first inquiries I asked her was if she had any additional information to tell me besides what was on the non-identifying information sheet. She responded by giving me nothing new, but the way in which she wrote it made me feel more emotionally connected to Joan. It was in a letter format, with paragraphs. It was much more personal than the bullet points I had in my grasp. Here is what she wrote me:

Rebecca -

Here is the background information that was previously sent to you. I hope that you find it helpful.

Background Information for Rebecca

It was indicated in the record that your birthmother did not want to give any information about her parents. She did report that she had a brother but did not state his age, occupation, or education.

Your birthmother's name is Joan. At the time she was known to our agency she was 5'10" tall and weighed 160 lbs. Joan has brown hair, brown eyes and a fair skin complexion. Joan is of Polish descent and was brought up in the Catholic faith.

Joan was not aware of her pregnancy until she entered the emergency room for delivery. Joan was 40 years old when you were born. She was a single woman struggling herself. She felt that she would have difficulty raising a child on her own. Joan believed that the best thing that she could do for you was to place you in a home with two loving parents.

Joan was employed as a bartender and enjoyed swimming and horseback riding. She was a smoker and smoked about 1 pack of cigarettes/day.

Your birthfather's name is Richard. Your birthfather and birthmother had a casual relationship. He was not aware of your birthmother's pregnancy and she was not able to give a lot of information about him. He was 6'1" tall and weighed approximately 200lbs. He enjoyed boating and sailing. He is of Irish descent.

I had also sent the social worker a list of questions I did not have the answers to. She answered the best she could, and I discovered Joan was born in Passaic County, New Jersey which I never knew. Throughout my various, numerous emails to the social worker, I discovered bits and pieces of Joan that I was hopeful I would be able to use to discover who she was.

Email: Bits and Pieces of Information:

Rebecca Tillou 11/30/2012 06:30 AM

Hey. So, I am aware you can only give out certain information. I am going to propose a list of questions, and any you can answer, I would greatly appreciate it.

1. What COUNTY was Joan born in? What CITY was she born in? Passaic County

2. What are her parents' first names? We were never given this information

3. What is her brother's first name? Any other siblings? We were never given this information

4. What bar/restaurant did she work at? we were not told

5. Did she have any other children when I was born? It does not appear that she had any other children at the time

of your birth.

6. Was she ever married before I was born? no

7. Did she actually graduate high school? this is not known

8. What county did she go to high school, what city? this is not known

9. What is the name of the high school she went to? unknown

10. Do you know if she is still in New Jersey? the letter that I sent out was in NJ, but we did not get a response so it is unknown

11. Are you able to attempt contact with her and see if she has a desire to meet me? we tried to make contact and did not get a response.

Thank you for your time, Rebecca

To: Rebecca Tillou

Subject: Re: Requesting Information

Sent: Mon, Dec 3, 2012 4:20:22 PM

Rebecca -

I can so see your desire to know more information and get all the pieces to your story, which I believe is everyone's right. I do not have all those pieces and cannot fill the blanks in for you. We have sent a letter to the last known address which never came back to us, but we did not receive a response from Joan. I will see if I can answer some of these questions for you that you have written below. At the time of your birth, it indicates that she was distressed and did not want to give a lot of information. We do not know all the details of her life and what was happening for her.

In addition to emailing the social worker, I decided to go online and find out what groups were out there that may be able to help me search. I had recently become a member of the All-Adoptee Group on Yahoo that was run by Sherrie Eldridge and Beth Willis Miller. This group told me to sign up with The ALMA Society (The Adoptees'

Liberty Movement Association). I went onto their website and sent them a check to become a part of their society. I also sent them the non-identifying information I had on Joan. They emailed me a list of all the Joans in the United States born on my birth mom's birthday, August 11, 1940. They had used DOBsearch.com (Concert Technologies, 2014) which is a website one can utilize to find names if you type in a date of birth, and you can also find dates of birth if you type in a name. Well, forty three names appeared on my computer screen when I opened up that first email from The ALMA society. I just kept staring at this extensive list of names, thinking one of them had to be my birth mom. Throughout my individual search, I would keep in touch with one of the ALMA members via email, and tell her of the Joans I had eliminated and which ones I was considering. This website was very useful. They had examples of letters written to birthmothers, in addition to the dos and don'ts of searching for your birth family, and some tips to follow if you do find them. ALMA sent me to the International Soundex Reunion Registry, also known as ISRR (International Soundex Reunion Registry, 1975). I followed the same steps I had for ALMA, only this time I didn't get a list of names. The way this registry works is that it runs searches based on the information I gave them about myself and Joan and sees if there are any words, phrases and dates that match. I also joined every adoption search site I could find online, and inputted my information and Joan's information.

I would go into my email every day, hoping to see an email from ISRR or any of the numerous adoption reunion registries I joined, stating, "we found a match! " After two weeks of nothing, ISRR and the other registries faded into the background in my world of searching.

For the next 6 months, I took each of the forty three names from ALMA and inputted them into 411.com (White Pages, 1998-2014). I wrote down addresses and phone numbers. One by one, I would dial the numbers. Each time, my heartbeat would quicken. I would feel shaky, as I waited for a voice on the other end. I think I got in touch by phone with 30 of the Joans or one of their family members. Many of the people were genuinely kind, they listened as I sputtered who I was and who I was looking for, sounding like a broken faucet. Many of them had true disappointment in their voice as they told me they were not my birth mom. I also utilized a website called Pipl.com (Pipl, 2006-2014). You can type in a first and last name, and a state if you want, and it will bring up all different web pages associated with that name. This website was useful for one Joan I searched who had the same date of birth as my birth mom. Pipl.com found a photo of her a few years back, at a musical convention. I sought this Joan out, and discovered she had musical talent. I was going to discard her immediately, because I have no musical talent whatsoever, unless you count my nightly renditions of *Row,*

Row Row Your Boat. I decided to keep her and research a little more because Pipl.com produced a photo that made me wonder, maybe we were related. We both had round faces and black hair. She was heavier than me though, and I did end up crossing her name off after not being able to locate a number or current address for her. It may have been my birth mom, but with so many other names to attend to, I figured I could always go back to her if I felt she was the only possible match.   Now, for those Joans I didn't locate a phone number for, I had addresses, and I sent each of them a personalized letter:

To Whom It May Concern:

Hi. My name is Rebecca. I am in search of my birth mom, her name is Joan, and she was born on August 11, 1940. She was born in Passaic County, New Jersey, and she has a polish sounding last name. I don't know her last name though. She is of the Catholic faith, and of Polish descent. She has one brother. I was born in Ridgewood New Jersey on January 12, 1980, and my birth mom was living in Bergen County, New Jersey at that time. If you received this letter, it is because in my internet search, I found that there was a Joan with a polish last name at this address, or possibly related to someone at this address.

Joan was a bartender (I am assuming in New Jersey close to Ridgewood) and felt she was not in a position to raise a child. She was 39 years old when she had me and claims she didn't know she was pregnant until she was in the delivery room. I know she enjoyed swimming and horseback riding, had a high school education, and was unmarried. At the time of my birth she was thin, 5 foot 10 inches tall, with brown hair and brown eyes. My father's name is Richard, he is Irish and likes boating and Sailing. He also has brown hair, brown eyes and was 6 feet tall in 1980. This is all I know. I was given a piece of paper with only this information on it.

I think about Joan often, and thank her for making the choice she made. I always feel like I have a void in my life. I look at my two little boys, and I wonder what parts of them look like Joan. I look in the mirror, and I see a stranger. I wonder if I look like her.

***Attached is a picture of me recently, taken June 24, 2012. If you see any resemblance to someone you may have seen, or know, or know somebody that may know of her…if you can maybe find out if she ever had a baby girl…I understand if it is just too awkward.

***If you are not my birth mother, or do not know her, or someone that may be her, if you wouldn't mind emailing me, calling me, or sending back a short note stating the same, so I may continue my search for my past. Thank you for your time ☺

Yours Truly,

Rebecca

Each one that received a letter got in touch with me. They either responded by paper, phone, and a select few responded via email. When I received a letter back I always had a glimmer of hope. It was similar to that packet you wait for when you apply to college. If the letter was thin, I opened it thinking it wasn't Joan, because I hoped if it was, the envelope would've been thicker with photos. I had letters emailed to me blessing me on my journey, and of course I had the one family that wrote me a letter stating, "Madam, Our family does not have a clue who your mother is or why you would be contacting us, none of us have ever heard of her. Please do not call, write or contact us in any manner." I guess being too forward with three phone messages and a letter can be seen as being a creeper. Oh well, one negative experience didn't deter me.

I also became very familiar with online obituaries. If I could not find information on a name, I would search obituaries. There were a handful of times that I was able to cross off a name because I would find her obituary, and based on the information I had for Joan regarding her family, the information did not match.

I remember one of the forty three Joans I researched I discovered through the internet that she had connections to horse racing. On the sheet of non-identifying information, my birth mom had written that she enjoyed horseback riding, so I thought for sure I had a match! I contacted a race track that this Joan was associated to. I divulged my journey to the lady on the other end of the phone. She asked me what I knew of the name I was inquiring about, and I quickly read off the address I had for her, and which stable she owned. I told her I didn't have a phone number. This lady, who after the phone call I deemed an angel in disguise, whispered a phone number to me. She then disclosed how her sister adopted a child, and she understood my desire to know my past. The last thing she told me was if anyone asked where I got the phone number, I was not to mention her name. I eventually did make contact with that Joan and her daughter. Her daughter contacted me a few weeks later, after I had left a message on her mom's voicemail and sent her a letter. She proceeded to explain that her mother Joan was very hard of hearing so she did not listen to her voicemail. She then told me that her mom read my letter, and wished she could've helped me. They were sincere, honest individuals whom I was glad to have met. Through my search for my birth mom, I learned there are many people in this world with warm hearts and blessed souls.

I familiarized myself with a social security website where you can type in a first and last name and if that person passed away, they may show up on this website. I used it with the list of Joans born on August 11, 1940. I was able to rule out a handful this way. At this moment in my search, I decided to take a chance, and I emailed the social worker and asked her to utilize the social security website and type in Joan's name. She emailed me back and said she had used the site and Joan was not on it. I remember I became so excited, because in my mind, that was proof she was alive…somewhere. I just had to find out where she was hiding.

I had this idea when I was searching for Joan that I would contact bars in New Jersey and see if any owners or employees had ever had a Joan work at their establishment. I went with bars in Passaic and Bergen county, and I would google search the bars and only contact those that had been around since the 1970's. Some of the bars were no longer in existence, while others were too busy to be bothered with a girl following a dream. Two bars actually took down my information and gave it to the owners. The owners of those two bars returned my call, and advised me that they were unable to help me, but wished me luck. One bar owner had relocated to Florida. I knew this because I looked up his name on 411.com (White Pages, 1998-2014) and found a number in Florida. I contacted him, and him and his wife told me that they did have a Joanie work for them, but the age was not correct for her to be my birth mother. I thanked them for their time and ended the phone call. Another bar employee told me to call back during the week around 2:30 pm. There were regulars who drank there every day, and they knew the bars around the area and the people that had worked in them back in the early 1980s. I made a phone call during the week at 2:30. The employee put me on hold while she asked the regulars if they had ever known of a Joan working as a bar tender or a waitress. The answers were all a resounding no. I reached out to some bars via Facebook and email. Many never responded, but I did hear back from the owner of one bar, who felt for me. He said there had been a Joan who worked for his bar years ago when his father was the owner. Unfortunately, she would be around 80 years old at the time I made contact with the bar. After this piece of information, feeling I was hitting too many dead ends, I decided to put the bars aside for a while, and stick to the names I had and the social worker.

At the end of a six month search, the response from all forty three Joans was a unanimous no. The last response

I received was by letter. It stated that she wished she could help me, but she had lived in Florida her entire life. She blessed me and wished me luck. I finished reading that letter as I slowly descended onto my couch and sighed. Within that sigh were feelings of frustration, sadness and helplessness. I had thoughts that I wasn't meant to know my birth mom and my roots. With a heavy heart, which at the same time felt empty, I stopped searching. There were a sea of names, and somewhere floating among them was Joan's full name.

Chapter Six

The Obsession Continues

I took a hiatus from my search for about three days, and then I pulled out the sheet of non-identifying information. I started to think maybe Joan's date of birth was typed incorrectly. My blood type on the non-identifying sheet had been wrong, so it was possible. Since beginning this search, my mind was constantly in a search mode. I went online and looked up typewriters used in the early 1980s, since my non-identifying information was typed up in 1980. I enlarged photos of the typewriter keys, and wrote down what numbers were in close proximity to numbers 8, 11, 4 and 0. The keys on a typewriter are the same layout as a computer. My mind raced with thoughts, "Maybe her date of birth was 8/12/1940 or 7/12/1940, or maybe 9/12/1940…what about 9/11/1940?!" Who knew number combinations and permutations would come back to haunt me after middle school math class? I replayed my method of operation from before using www.DOBsearch.com (Concert Technologies, 2014) and www.411.com (White Pages, 1998-2014), only I plugged in other "possible" dates of birth. No letters were sent this round, only phone calls. This portion of my journey ended empty handed. I emailed the adoption agency and asked the social worker to peek in my file and relay back to me if Joan had written the same date of birth I had. My mind started to whirl even more. I asked her to look to see how her name was spelled and if she had a middle initial. I was somewhat surprised she emailed me back because I felt I was digging for answers I was not entitled to.

Email: Spelling of Name

Rebecca -

I looked through the file again and there is a signature that shows that we have the same spelling. The birthdate is the same everywhere I looked. She did not have a lot of contact with our agency and did not provide much information.

From:

To:

Subject: RE: Two Questions

Sent: Wed, Mar 13, 2013 5:27:15 PM

Well, ok then. Let's stick to the original facts, "First name Joan, no middle initial, date of birth 8/11/1940." From that moment on, I looked at the non-identifying information at face value. Now, the sheet stated that Joan was of Polish descent. Hmm…I bombarded the social worker with another question answer session.

Ok, my first question is, I had written down that Joan had a brother...is that what you have as well? I only ask because I wasn't sure when you wrote unknown if that was in response to other siblings, or a brother as well

Second question: Should I be searching for a Polish sounding last name? Hey...I had to try right? :)

From:

To: Rebecca Tillou

Subject: Re: Two Questions

Sent: Fri, Dec 7, 2012 3:48:48 PM

Rebecca

I looked through again and there is one notation "has

brother" in the chart. It appears that the Bethany worker

met your birth mom for the first time after you were born.

This may be why there is not a lot of information in the

file. She was of Polish descent, so you can assume that she

had a Polish sounding last name:

There it was, in print. The biggest clue I would receive

throughout my search: *She was of Polish descent, so you*

can assume that she had a Polish sounding last name. I

went back onto DOBsearch.com (Concert Technologies,

2014), and looked up Joans with Polish last names. I had to

limit the search somehow because the amount of Joans in

the entire United States with Polish last names was too many to keep my sanity. I decided I would stick to the East Coast. Once again, I printed out letters and made phone calls. Once again, I was let down gently with every contact made.

I felt defeated. I wasn't sure how many more times I could let myself feel defeated. I was looking to enlist help. Free help, if it was possible. Through the internet, I found a group of individuals who call themselves *search angels*. Who are they? They are true angels that search for your past and clues to who you are. What do they ask for in return? A successful story they can use as testimony when others come to them in need of an angel. I ended up with two search angels who became my wings that lifted me up when I was falling.

"You can't know what you don't know." That is one of the angel's mottos. Her name is Diana. It is that motto that became ingrained in my mind, and helped keep my spirits up throughout my journey.

Now that I had Diana to help me out and utilize sources I did not have at my fingertips, I decided to go back to a name I had crossed off a few months ago, based on the fact she was a JoAnn, not a Joan...JoAnn Scoff...born 8/11/1940. She was born in Newark, New Jersey. Diana had been working with me, and found 2 pictures of JoAnn's daughter. We both saw a resemblance, as did my best friend. It was hard, because we saw what we wanted to see, but there were also facts. She had a Polish maiden last name, her date of birth was the same as Joan's, and they had similar hair and eye color. I googled her name, and I found her name in a Catholic Church bulletin. Another similarity between my birth mother and Joann! Her name was in the bulletin every month in memory of her. She had passed away in 2006. I continued to google her name, and I came across a 3 mile race in which a boy had donated money in her honor. I found her daughter's Facebook page and I sent a message. I never heard back. In the time I was waiting to hear back, I googled what I thought was JoAnn's maiden last name. I called the phone number I found. It turned out to be JoAnn's ex-husband's phone number. This man surprisingly was very open with me. He told me they got married after dating for a couple years. He discussed with me how she did not want children, and he already had children. The timeline between when Joan had me and when this JoAnn got married would mean *if* she was my birth mom, then she had a baby before they were married. Her ex-husband got quiet after I offered this possibility. He then said JoAnn was not like that, she would've told him, and he would've been able to tell she was pregnant. He then told me she would not have had an affair, so I most likely was not her daughter. I was not ready to cross her name off. I thanked him, and hung up the phone. I decided to email the social worker. I wrote to her, explaining who I had found, and how I thought she was my birth mother even though her name was spelled differently. She emailed me back and advised that she really did not think JoAnn Scoff was my birth mother. I took her at her word, grabbed a Sharpie, and put a dark line through her name.

Diana decided to search for Joan on Classmates.com (1995-2014, classmates.com). We had her date of birth, and we decided to assume she graduated on time in 1958. Given that she was born in Passaic County, Diana pulled up each Passaic County school yearbook from 1958 that was on Classmates.com. From there, she searched for Joans with Polish last names. She would send me the yearbook photos of the girls she felt resembled me in some way. Whether it was a similar chin tilt or a similar nose. She even scrutinized eye shape! Diana would put each photo she found in an excel spread sheet next to a photo of me, and in the columns she would write her notes.

Diana also had access to Ancestry.com. Within Ancestry.com, she went to Passaic county neighborhoods in 1959 and 1960; two years post Joan's graduation date. All of the Joans she located were married. We eliminated them because although Joan could've gotten married, we decided to stick with non-married so as not to overwhelm ourselves. We had enough Joans' to sift though. Diana sent me a photo of a Joan in which she saw similarities to me, and I didn't really see any, but I trusted her ideas and input, so I walked with her down the path of possibility. I found an address based on her name, and sent out a letter. I received an email back, explaining that the lady who was emailing me was Joan's granddaughter. She explained in her email she was very close to Joan, and they had grown up with a close grandma-granddaughter bond. She wrote that Joan was a very private person, and grew up very shy and closed off from people. I read those statements and I thought it could be my birth mother. Maybe she became closed off after having to place a child for adoption. Her granddaughter told me she would see if an opportunity ever arose to ask Joan if she ever gave birth to a child and gave it up for adoption. I emailed back that I appreciated the assistance. A couple weeks went by, and I received an email in my inbox from Joan's granddaughter. She said she had given it a lot of thought, and had not asked her grandmother if she ever gave a child up, but she asked other family members, and they said there was no way. I emailed her back and thanked her for taking the time to write to me. She told me to keep in touch, as she wanted to know about the turn out of my search. I had a few women who I had spoken to regarding this search who told me to keep in touch. Throughout this journey, I had begun to have a following. I felt a little bit like a celebrity.

One by one the photos got crossed off. I decided to see what other online yearbook sites were available. I came across E-yearbook.com (Digital Data Online, Inc, 2005-

2013). I looked up all 1958 yearbooks from Passaic county schools. By this time, any Joan with a Polish last name resembled me in my mind. She could be blue eyed and blonde, or have red hair with freckles and I would star her photo as a possibility. My eyes and my heart were desperate and so hopeful, what my family and friends would see as clearly no resemblance I would think could be Joan. With every photo I saw, every name I wrote down, I wondered if my search had ended. I would wonder each time if I had found the key to the locked door of my past.

Weeks went by and photos continued to dwindle. I decided to try an avenue that some people I had spoken to through Sherrie Eldridge's Yahoo Adoptee group had tried. DNA testing. I originally didn't even entertain the thought, because how would DNA testing work if I didn't have another half to test their DNA? I was told to join a DNA Yahoo group to get a better idea of what DNA testing can discover about a person. I found out that DNA testing could find out my ethnic makeup. I already knew I was Polish and Irish, but I was not too certain on the Irish part, given my birth mom did not really know the man who she claimed was my father. I also found out that some of the DNA tests would put your DNA into a bank, and if there were any matches made, they would advise. The neat thing is that sometimes matches occurred with distant relatives, sometimes six or seven times removed. I figured it was worth doing. There were a few DNA test kits out there, and after researching each one, I decided to go with 23andme. They were having a deal online, so I ordered a kit for $100.00. While I was waiting to receive the DNA kit, I researched the rules and regulations. I found that if you lived in New York State like myself, you were not allowed to ship your saliva out through New York. The New York department of health believes a physician is needed for DNA testing. New York State does allow you to have the DNA kit mailed to you and then one just mails it out in another state. I received the DNA kit after about 10 days. I had to register myself on their website, so I would be able to follow my results and any matches they may find. I decided I would do the test and have my parents mail it out of South Carolina where they live. Well, my parents came to visit multiple times, and each time they left empty handed. I always forgot to do it, and to ask them to mail it for me. I think in the back of my mind I had figured nothing would come of it, simply because nobody had reached out to find me in other ways such as mail, email or phone. So there the DNA kit sat. I felt secure knowing I had it in my possession, if the urge ever struck me to go through with it. I finally did perform the DNA test and the results came up with second and third cousins, but none of us can figure out how we are related. The DNA test did not lead me to any biological siblings, cousins, aunts or uncles like I had hoped.

In the midst of waiting for my DNA results I decided I would peruse Classmates.com, and see what I could find without actually having to join the site. I decided I would search Bergen County, New Jersey high school yearbooks. Bergen County is where I was born and adopted, and I thought maybe Joan's high school alma mater was there. The week of May 6, 2013 I was looking at Bogota High School's class of 1958 yearbook. Bogota is a small town in Bergen County. I came across a girl's photo and I was about to turn the page, but then I read her name. "Chanowski. Joan Chanowski." I studied the photo. I clicked on the photo at least 10 times to enlarge it, but all that did was make the photo blurrier. I looked at Joan's face, and stated out loud that she was manly looking. I clicked to the next page, looked at a few more photos, and was going to call it a night, but first I wanted my husband to look at the picture of Joan Chanowski. My husband Jason walked into the computer room. I had him look at the photo. I kept looking at the photo and looking at him to see his reaction. I had twinges of nerves in my stomach, because I saw something in Joan Chanowski's photo that reminded her of me, and I was hoping he would say he thought I had found my birth mom. Instead, he told me he saw some similarities but nothing extraordinary. Then he left the room. I took a last look, pushed my chair away from the computer, and went to bed. It took me a while to fall asleep that night, because I kept seeing Joan Chanowski's face in front of my closed eyes. I had not yet had a Joan keep me awake.

The next morning, I went downstairs to get into the shower. A gravitational force pulled me to the computer. I sat down and pulled up the photo of Joan Chanowski. It was a new day, my eyes were freshly rested. I stared at her. My heart started beating quicker, and I could feel my eyes widen. My mouth started to go dry. I felt like I did when I was in high school before a cross country meet. It was her.

Joan Chanowski was my birth mother. I was looking in a mirror, at my reflection. We had identical facial features: our nose, the shape of our eyes, our mouth, even our eyebrows were similar. I felt like I couldn't catch my breath. It was the first time in my life I had seen another woman who was my likeness. A trait many take for granted. A trait I couldn't believe I had finally discovered.

Joan was identical to my high school senior photos, except I was smiling, and she was serious. I emailed the photo out to my parents. My father had a classic response of, "Son of a bitch, I think she found her! "My mom replied, "This is not a coincidence." Another relative had thought I had gone to one of those old time photo shoots and dressed up in 1950s attire. Now, my husband has always been my voice of reason. I am an extremely impulsive individual, and I found out a few years later this trait is because of a decision Joan made. I get an idea, I want to make it reality and I don't want anyone to tell me otherwise. I had my husband take a look at Joan Chanowski's photo the morning I decided she was my birth mom. He looked at her face, and then he looked at me. He told me what he had told me the night before, that he saw similarities, but wasn't sure it was her. He held to his opinion as he didn't want me to get my hopes up just to have them shattered. I would ask him every day from then on if he thought Joan Chanowski was my birth mom. Until I had confirmation 3 weeks later, my husband would not waiver from his first impression.

Chapter Seven

A Name, A Connection

JOAN CHANOWSKI

"Joan" . . . "That's the way the cookie crumbles" . . . dislikes short boys . . . keeps her mind on what she is doing . . . wants to be a secretary . . . one of our taller girls.

There I was. I had a name. I was 100% positive Joan Chanowski gave birth to me that winter morning in 1980. Hmm…so now what? I had been so entrenched in searching for a name, and now I had a name and a face. I googled her name, hoping to find links to her Facebook page, maybe a race she ran the week before, maybe a neighborly deed she did that got put in the local paper. I found a webpage for Bogota High School, and located her graduating class, 1958. I decided I would add Joan's photo to the web page, and under the comments section I wrote about my journey and who Joan was. I was hopeful someone else on the web page would reach out to me, and be able to disclose some information on her. I never received any responses to Joan's photo or my story, so I decided to search for the addresses and phone numbers of Bogota High School alumni of 1958. I sent out letters and made phone calls. I heard back from one person only and that was from his wife. She left me a voicemail saying her husband had no clue who Joan Chanowski was.

I kept searching for anything that would give me a glimpse into Joan as a person, not just a name. I kept rolling her name around on my tongue. There was this little voice that kept resonating in the depths of my mind. It was telling me I had seen Joan Chanowski's name before. I opened my black pseudo leather binder with all of my findings in it from this adoption search. I found nothing with Joan's name on it. I feverishly clicked into the emails I had been collecting. This is what I found:

From: Rebecca Tillou

To

Subject: FW: ok

Sent: Wed, Dec 19, 2012 7:36:27 PM

Am I even close to being on the right track? Sowinski, Watkowski, Zilinski, Dombrowski, *Chanowski*...Passaic and Bergen Counties. Those are what I have it narrowed down to

From: Sent: Wednesday, December 19, 2012 2:33 PM

To: Rebecca Tillou

Subject: Re: ok

Rebecca, I am very sorry, but I cannot tell you either way.

My hand started shaking as I scrolled down through the email. I had her name all along! I am a strong believer that everything happens for a reason. Sometimes we know the reason, sometimes we do not. I still don't know why I wasn't keyed into researching Joan Chanowski more after I wrote that email, but whatever the reason, I now knew Joan Chanowski was my birth mother, and I now all I needed was a phone number and an address.

I returned to DOBsearch.com (Concert Technologies, 2014). I found Joan Chanowski's last known address and phone number and picked up my cell phone. The numbers in front of me were blurry. Why were my cell phone number keys all blurry? Then I looked at my hand. It was trembling, making the phone shake. All of this time I kept coming face to face with doors that had no key, and now I was in front of a door with a key that should work. I dialed the numbers slowly. Then I took a deep breath. There was a half ring and then the familiar, "We are sorry, but that number is not in service. Please check the number and dial again." Then the dial tone. I clicked end on my cell phone. My next and last idea was to mail a letter to Joan Chanowski. I printed out the letter, drove to the post office, and slid it down the cold, hard, metal door into the blue abyss.

I am one of those people who can't just sit around. I am constantly thinking of things to do to keep myself busy. I figured why not send out letters to every Chanowski in the United States. So, off to work I went. I scoured 411.com (White Pages, 1998-2014) and sent out letters to each Chanowski that had an address.

To Whom It May Concern:

*My name is Rebecca Tillou, and I am searching for Joan Chanowski who graduated from Bogota High School in Bergen NJ in 1958. I believe she was born in 1940 in Passaic County NJ and passed away on February 11, 1999 in Paterson, NJ. She did have one brother, although I do not know his first name or if he was older or younger. I am doing a genealogy project and I have discovered I am related to the Chanowski's, specifically Joan Chanowski. I was born in Ridgewood New Jersey on January 12, 1980. I was put up for adoption and adopted on February 13, 1980. I would appreciate a call back, email, or a letter. Even if you do not know of her, please contact me so I can cross her off the list of possible relatives. Thank you for helping me with my project. ***I am sending this to* *another spelling of Chanowski, Chrzanowski, because I am*

not having luck with anybody with the last name

Chanowski ever hearing of Joan☺

My email is:

My phone number is

My address is:

***BELOW is a picture of Joan on the left in 1958 (her

senior picture), and me (June 2013): If the pictures

resonate with you, please let me know.

JOAN CHANOWSKI
"Joan" . . "That's the way the cookie crumbles" . . dislikes short boys . . . keeps her mind on what she is doing . . . wants to be a secretary . . . one of our taller girls.

I also attempted phone contact with those that had phone numbers. I remember getting in contact with Barrie Chanowski in Florida, who answered the phone suspiciously. She was hesitant to give any information, and when she did give information, it was minimal. I asked her if she had ever resided in New Jersey, and she advised years ago. She told me her late husband John grew up in New Jersey but she had never heard about a Joan

Chanowski. I thanked her for her time and hung up the phone.

A couple days later, as I was still trying to wrap my head around Joan Chanowski, I got a Facebook message from Elaine, one of my search angels. She asked if she could call me. I responded *of course*, and then my phone rang. I answered the phone, and Elaine told me she had a piece of information for me on Joan Chanowski. My heart skipped a beat. "You know, you can't really be sure she is your mom from a photo," Elaine's voice came over the receiver, calm yet business like. I responded that sometimes that is true, but in this case, Joan Chanowski was without a doubt my birth mom. There was silence on the other end. I thought I heard Elaine take a breath. Then, the words came through the receiver, "Well, Joan Chanowski is dead."

Chapter Eight

From Death to Dynamics

I felt like someone had tapped me behind the knees, making me unsteady. I quickly composed myself, and asked Elaine how she knew that. She went on to tell me that after I had written on Facebook about finding my birth mom, she had been rooting around on the web, trying to locate information on Joan. She wanted to see if Joan had passed away, based on the fact we could not find much information on her. She came across a web page for Passaic County Surrogate Court Index, typed in Joan's name and it appeared on the screen, with February 11, 1999 as her date of death. My mind reeled back to that date, because I knew it well. It was the same exact date and year I had broken up with the track coach. Two losses in my life on the same day, discovered years apart. The world has some strange coincidences. I waited for the tears to start falling, the sobs to creep up into my throat. None of that happened. I told Elaine I thought this was a possibility since nobody seemed to be able to find out much about her. Elaine and I said our goodbyes, and I started dialing my mom's number. I didn't feel at that moment. I wasn't sad, I wasn't disappointed, I felt…nothing. My mom answered the phone. "Joan is dead." My voice started to crack. It took the voice of familiarity and support to let my feelings surface. My mom felt for me. She said she was sorry. I told her I was ok, it didn't really affect me. I had always been good at pushing my emotions down into the depths below my heart. My mom's words, although not many, were so sincere, so kind, and so meaningful. I said goodbye and hung up. I sat down on the couch in the basement and closed my eyes. Ever since I was six years old I had visions of meeting my birth mom. I had visions of us running towards one another on a hill, hair flowing, and then embracing. I used to imagine her calling me up on the phone and stating who she was and that she wanted to meet me and my family. Those visions broke into little pieces, and dissolved amongst my tears that finally started to fall.

On May 13, 2013, while my family was having dinner, my phone rang. I researched the number, it was from Pennsylvania. I debated about calling the number back or letting it go because no voicemail was left. I decided to call back and a man answered. "Is this Rebecca? My name is Tom Chanowski, I got your letter. Weird thing is, I just moved. I don't live at that address anymore. My mail is still being forwarded." He asked me how I knew Joan. I got all flustered and I started sputtering like a faucet again. I told him in a quiet, cautious voice, "She is my birth mother." His reaction was not what I had anticipated. I expected him to drop the phone or say, "Oh my goodness!" Or reply using the infamous words of my father, "Son of a bitch!" Instead, he simply stated, "Oh," and that he was Joan's first cousin. I was speechless. I was

on the phone with my biological second cousin! I first

asked him if he knew a Barrie Chanowski. He started to

laugh, a manly, gruff laugh, and said that was his sister in

law. His brother had died a few years before and his wife

had remained in Florida. The fact that Joan was never

mentioned to Barrie by Tom's brother or Tom himself

didn't sit well with me. I thought she would've come up in

conversation at some point. I then told Tom Joan had

passed away in 1999. His response was simply that he was

sorry to hear that. I took from his reply that Joan and he

were not closely knit.

Tom then went on to explain the dynamics of the

Chanowski last name. Joan's last name was originally

spelled Chrzanowski. Thomas' last name was originally

spelled Chrzanowski as well, but his father had the r and

the z taken out (I found out later by my biological uncle

that Thomas' father had been a teacher, and it was easier

for the kids to spell the surname without the r and the z).
The Chrzanowski's all grew up in Bloomfield, New
Jersey. Joan's brother's name is Mark Chrzanowski. At
one point in my search, I had googled different spellings of
Chanowski. I had found the Chrzanowski spelling, and I
had Mark's address and phone number written down. I
had been very overwhelmed at that point, and wanted to
stick to one spelling. So Mark's name was put aside into a
little folder. It is interesting how life comes full circle.
Thomas reminisced that he grew up a few blocks from
Mark, and they used to hang out together as boys usually
do, playing basketball and talking about anything and
nothing. He last saw Mark 15 years ago when Mark had a
convention in New York. Tom last saw Joan when he was
12 years old and she came to his house for a quick visit.

"Joan lived with the nuns." Tom stated these
words to me, and they were like an echo in my head. I
didn't hear anything else. I asked Tom what he meant by

that. He recalled that she lived with nuns, and didn't know for how long or why. I asked if her brother also lived with nuns, and he recalled that as far as he knew Mark had always lived with his father and grandmother. My mind was swishing with questions now, questions I had a feeling I would have to discover on my own, as Tom didn't know much about the personal life of Joan or her brother. I asked Tom why Joan had Chanowski spelled differently than Mark. He did not know, and I never did find out why. I assume maybe because Joan grew up with the nuns, it was easier to spell for the

Nuns given that they had to keep track of multitudes of children with different last names.

Throughout the conversation, Tom struck me as a sweet older gentleman who loved to chat about the past. He helped me piece my past together, the past I never knew, and for that I will be forever thankful. The last words Tom spoke to me during that phone call was Mark

Chrzanowski's address. I scribbled it down, thanked Tom

for helping me find answers, and ended the phone call.

Chapter Nine

Like Mother, Like Daughter

**The aftermath of the Joe Louis fight (my biological
grandfather down)**

January 11, 1937

The date was May 17, 2013; the time was 1:12 pm.

I was sitting at my desk at work, and I felt my desk

vibrating. I looked over and saw my phone was lighting

up, and a call was coming through. I recognized the 214

area code as a Texas area code. I had written down a phone

number of my Joan's brother Mark that I found on
Ancestry.com that had the same area code. I quickly
answered it. The man on the other line had a shaky, gruff,
uncertain voice. He introduced himself as Mark
Chrzanowski. He told me he received my letter, and
would help me in any way he could. Mark told me he
would give me the medical history of the Chrzanowski
family. After a few seconds of silence, Mark asked me,
"Just what is your relationship to Joan?" I hesitated,
because in the letter I had not stated I was Joan's daughter
only that I was related to the Chrzanowski's, specifically
Joan, and I was placed for adoption. I told him I was
Joan's biological daughter. His response was similar to his
Cousin Tom's in that he didn't act astounded. He told me
calmly he thought I was her daughter based on the photos I
sent him. He told me I had her eyes. I was waiting for him
to tell me he wanted nothing to do with me, and to hang up

the phone. Instead, he did the opposite. We ended up speaking for an hour and 10 minutes.

I sat down, pencil and paper in my hand. Mark proceeded to feed me all the medical history on his family, as I quickly jotted everything down. He started off by telling me everyone had strong teeth. It struck me as odd that those words were the first comments out of a man's mouth who was talking to a lady he has never spoken to before. That being said, I am 33 years old and never had a cavity. I guess my strong teeth are Chrzanowski teeth. He then told me the Chrzanowskis are tall, all standing about 6 feet or taller. Mark is 6 foot 4, his father was 6 foot 5, Joan was 5 foot 10, and his children and grandchildren are all tall. I sat, my phone pressed fast to my ear, listening intently to every word. So, my long, slender arms and legs now make sense. My super narrow banana peel feet and ET like fingers I understand. My height of 5 foot 2 inches is lost on me though. Either my biological father was not my biological father, or the alcohol Joan ingested blessed me with a short stature of 5 foot 2 inches.

Mark spoke about my biological grandfather, and how he had passed away at 48 years old of a massive heart attack. He had multiple heart attacks while he was alive. He used to eat one large pizza by himself with quarts of beer to wash them down: for breakfast! Mark told me how he also had cardiac issues and had endured a couple heart attacks as well. Now, after 33 years of wondering, I knew where my elevated cholesterol came from. I walked away from this conversation knowing I now had an important piece of medical history that could help steer me and my children away from the hazardous paths lined with cardiac issues. Another piece placed into the puzzle of my past. As I was speaking with Mark, I was envisioning my non-identifying information. "Nothing significant in health history." At first, I was angry, but that anger would quickly dissipate, as I learned why Joan had written *nothing significant in health history.* Joan was not privy to the health history of her relatives. As I would learn, she was in the same position I was in, until I located her family. A woman I had never met, but we were genetically related, and we had both been kept in the dark for many years about our health history. Why Joan lived in the dark regarding her family and health history would be revealed as the conversation with Mark and I continued.

During that first conversation with my biological uncle, Mark asked me, "So, you are my niece?" I replied, "Yea, I guess I am." He then told me he was elated to hear he had a niece. That made me feel warm inside and made me smile.

I felt extremely blessed at this moment. I had spoken to Mark's cousin Tom for a second time before talking to Mark, and he had spoken to his sister Karen. Karen had gone to my biological grandfather's funeral in 1963, and Mark and Joan were there. She recalled that there were raised voices between Mark and Joan and some sort of falling out ensued. I asked Mark about this conversation, and he stated there had not been a falling out. He remembered he last saw Joan at a bar where she worked in 1963. He thinks it was the Hillcrest Tavern in Paterson, New Jersey. Maybe Mark had some feelings of guilt, knowing he got to remain with the Chrzanowski family while his baby sister was sent off into the big, dark world…alone. Yet, there was no hesitation in Mark's words as he said how happy he was I had connected with him and that we were related.

Mark told me he has three children, Karen, Linda, and a son Kenny. I found out Linda and Linda's daughter ran cross country and track in high school, and my second cousin Tom's father also ran in high school. My mouth was smiling; my eyes were squinting from smiling so much. My high school career consisted of Cross Country and Track all 4 years. Running was innate, it was in my blood. Mark told me his granddaughter (Linda's daughter Andrea) received a full soccer scholarship and full academic scholarship to the University of Arkansas. He raved about how athletic and bright Andrea is. I immediately thought about my son Dominic. I told him my son Dominic started reading at 3 and a half, and Mark told me Andrea was the same when she was a toddler.   Now, I know my son gets his smarts from my husband and his gentle spirit and over sensitive nature from me, but now I know there is intelligence from my biological family that could've permeated into my son's genes. I continued to be amazed throughout the rest of my journey at the ability to connect a few of the leaves of me and my sons to my biological family tree.

After catching up on my genetics, I took a breath, closed my eyes, and told Mark I had some information about his sister, Joan. Mark got quiet, awaiting my words. I told Mark that Joan had passed away in February of 1999.

Mark was unaware of this. He didn't begin to cry, but just replied in a surprised tone, "I didn't know." He told me again the last time he saw Joan was in 1963. I was raised in a close knit family. Hearing Mark tell me that he hadn't seen his sister since 1963 floored me. Without me asking, Mark delved into a bit of the family history and the family dynamics. My biological grandfather's name was Boleslaw or William Chrzanowski. My biological grandmother's name was Ruth Wolff. My biological grandfather and grandmother had given birth to Mark, and when he was 10 months old, my biological grandmother skipped out. A couple years later my biological grandfather met up with my biological grandmother again in Buffalo, New York, and she became pregnant with Joan. After having Joan, Ruth ran out on her family again, never to be seen again. My biological grandfather was never around much. He was a professional small town boxer from Bloomfield, New Jersey who fought under the name Stanley (or Steve)

Ketchell. He fought big time boxers such as Joe Louis and James Braddock (Cinderella Man). When he wasn't competing in fights, he was making a living for his family doing odds and ends jobs, which included working for a bread company. Mark was pretty much raised by his grandmother. When Joan was born, she was sent to Immaculate Conception Orphanage in Lodi NJ. I have asked Mark since this first conversation on more than one occasion why she was sent away. He maintains that he is not sure. He was only a toddler when Joan was placed in the orphanage and his family never pulled him aside to explain why. Mark told me that he believes his grandmother didn't feel able to raise two children, and young ones at that, on her own. So Joan got sent away. It seemed like time stopped when I heard what happened to Joan. All noise seemed to cease. In my head, "Orphanage" was on repeat. When Mark apprised me of this piece of history, my heart dropped. Never had I envisioned this scenario. Like mother like daughter. An innocent child given to an orphanage; later I would discover she was never adopted. She was bounced around from foster home to foster home. Joan never married that I am aware of, and per Mark she worked as a cocktail waitress in a lounge bar. She never knew what it was to be a mother as she never had a stable mother figure. Joan's decision to place me for adoption meant I could've ended up in foster care for years like her, but she probably envisioned that would be better than living with a woman who was single, a drunk, worked in a bar, never had a mother and didn't know how to be one. It all makes sense now. My heart went out to her. The conversation ended with me telling Mark I would call every now and again to check up on him and his wife and his family. He told me that would be greatly appreciated. He thanked me and told me I had just brightened his days. I told him I felt the same, and hung up the phone.

As soon as the phone call ended, my mind was reeling. I wondered if I could find someone who attended Immaculate Conception back when Joan would've attended. I googled the orphanage, knowing full well the orphanage was no longer being used as such. I found that the building was still standing, and then I discovered the orphanage had a Facebook page. I went onto the page, and I decided to message some of the members. In my message, I explained who I was and my discovery of Joan Chanowski as my birth mother. I received a message back from a young woman, who was much younger than Joan, and she tentatively shared some of her experiences at the orphanage. Her messages had the shadows of past hurts. She said the orphanage was not a place she would want anyone to go. It wasn't horrible, but it was a sad place. One lady had posted on the Facebook site about how she remembered every weekend they would all clean themselves up and stand in a straight line. Families would go down the line of children and choose those that looked the cleanest, the prettiest and cutest to take to their home for the weekend. When I read this post, I got immediate visions of Joan, standing in a line of other girls, her beautiful wavy brown hair to her shoulders, wearing a dress. She looked serious in my mirage, no smile parted her lips. In her mind, she was hopeful she would be chosen for a weekend getaway, but overshadowing that hope were thoughts that she was not good enough, she was not deserving of love. I decided maybe this young woman on the Facebook page had a contact for someone who used to work at the orphanage. She ended up having contact information for a nun who used to work at the orphanage. I decided nothing could be lost by writing her a letter. I sent out a letter, and waited for a response. About a week later, I received a phone call from the nun I had contacted. She told me she had read my letter, and her heart was broken for my birth mother. She said I had been on an amazing journey, and she didn't remember Joan's name off hand, but she would search the orphanage records to see if she could unearth anything. She told me she would let me know if she came across any documents. A few days after our conversation, the nun called me again, and she apologized for not finding any papers on Joan. I appreciated her taking the time out of her busy schedule to search for the missing years of Joan's life. She assured me that Joan's life at the orphanage was one filled with love. I appreciated her telling me that. I am sure there was love in that orphanage, but I am not sure Joan knew what love was, or if she was aware of love. I am not sure she trusted anyone to love her.

So now, in just 3 weeks, I had found my birth mother's senior high school photo, discovered her full name, talked to her cousin, spoken to her brother, found out she is dead, and was an orphan. Ok, time to put away the detective hat and get back to reality…right? This is all I wanted, right? No. Once I knew she was dead, I wanted to know how she died.

Chapter Ten

Reality of the Past

I made the decision to try to order Joan's estate file in hopes of discovering how she passed away. It was easier to do than I anticipated. I didn't realize estate files are open to the public, for anyone's eyes to see. I sent a letter to Passaic Surrogate Court requesting her estate file. I found the address online. The court sent me a letter back advising they received my inquiry and then gave me a written breakdown of the file's contents and the price of each document. I sent money for the entire file and then waited impatiently. The cost was not as much as I thought, only $45!

The week of May 27, 2013, I crossed the street in front of our house and opened the mailbox. In the mailbox lay a yellow envelope. On the front it said Passaic County Surrogate Court. I ran inside and hastily opened the envelope. My palms felt sweaty, and I was afraid I would smear the documents. I sat down at our kitchen table. There was a *Certificate of Death* on the top of the mound of papers. I had no idea where to look for the cause of death. I scanned the document, my eyes squinting then widening, because the copy was not very clear. Then I saw it. "*Blunt force injury of head & neck, fall down stairs*." I never thought that would be her cause of death. I thought possibly a heart attack, a stroke… or maybe a car accident. I read that line out loud to my husband, and started laughing. He came over and read the certificate, and put his hand on my shoulder. My laughter turned into tears. This emotional roller coaster was allowing me to feel every emotion within seconds of one another. I told my husband that seeing in print how she passed away made it all more real. I saw the words and a grotesque visual permeated my mind.

Joan's Death Certificate

Ok, so now I knew how she died. I should've been able to put this paper away in a file folder with all of the search documents, and close this chapter in my life. I was not even close to being able to do that. Now I wanted to know why she fell down the stairs. On the certificate was the identity of the executor of the Estate, Faye. Next to her name, was "relationship to the decedent," and there was the word "friend."

I pulled out the chair in front of my computer, sat down, and pulled up 411.com (White Pages, 1998-2014). I typed in the name of Joan's executor, and only came up with her name. No address found. I went to a social security website where you can search death records by name. I typed in Faye's name and discovered she had passed away. I was disappointed and sad. I had hoped to get insight into Joan's personality, her daily life and her deepest secrets. I had to keep believing everything happens for a reason. I continued to search through the packet of information in the estate file. I came across a hand written will for Joan, written on June 1, 1992, and signed by Faye and another lady, Darlene. The will stated Joan wanted to leave her possessions to Faye and Darlene, as she had no relatives to speak of. My heart sank, because Joan had a brother, but she didn't consider him a relative. She was bounced around from family to family her entire life, and I speculate that she didn't consider anyone to be family. I wished at that moment she was alive, so I could embrace her, and tell her we would always be relatives. I felt I was truly blessed to have been adopted into a family of love. I couldn't fathom living Joan's life of what appeared to be loneliness and uncertainty.

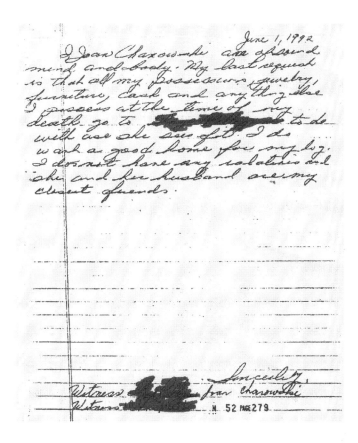

Joan's Will

Within the estate file, there were court documents regarding a civil case over the validity of Joan's will that was written in 1992. The will turned out to be written by Faye, and witnessed by Faye and her daughter. When questioned in court why Faye wrote the will and not Joan herself, Faye explained that Joan's handwriting was illegible most of the time, and she had asked that Faye write up the will. Apparently Joan had asked multiple times for her will to be written. Faye had no idea why Joan was so insistent on writing a will because she didn't have much to leave behind, except some jewelry and her beloved dogs. Looking over the documents, I wonder if maybe the alcohol had gotten to Joan's brain and made her a little unwell and paranoid, and she wanted to make sure the few possessions she had, especially her dogs, went into hands she trusted.

I discovered through reading the estate file that Joan had a life insurance policy in the amount of $30,000, and once the attorneys for the insurance company heard she had passed away, they contacted Faye to see if Joan had a will, and questioned her about Joan's relatives. Faye explained that Joan had never mentioned any relatives, as was also written in the will. She immediately mailed the will to the insurance company. Faye then received a summons and complaint regarding the hand written will, stating it was not valid because it was hand written. Faye attended court, and it was decided after Faye's testimony that the hand written will would be considered valid. Joan's life insurance payout was given to Faye, and the case was closed. The amount of information I came across I was not expecting. One question would be answered, and five more would appear. I question why Joan would even have a life insurance policy. Through Faye's testimony regarding the will, I discovered Joan's only jobs were briefly at a phone company, a brief stent at a bank, and then she was a bar tender. Maybe one of her foster families opened an account for her. Whatever the reason for Joan wanting a will and having a life insurance policy, I just hope everything was done in an honest manner, and out of love. I hope nobody took advantage of Joan's situation, a lonely, single girl just trying to make it through another day.

I figured I would research Darlene's identity, to possibly get a glimpse into Joan's life and who she was. I looked her up on the internet, and found her address and phone number. I called her and left a message. I also found her on Facebook and sent her a message. A week later, I was pulling into my driveway from work, and I saw I missed a call. I returned the call, and Darlene answered, telling me she was Faye's daughter. She then told me, "Rebecca, you are a blast from the past." I had been walking down to the serene creek in the back of my house to have the phone conversation. I stopped mid trek and almost dropped the phone. In a meek voice, I replied, "Wait, you knew about me?" Darlene recalled "I remember the day you came along." She laughed and said, "Rebecca, your birth was a comedy of errors."

She then went on to tell me that Joan was an alcoholic. Her mother Faye owned a bar named The Copper Penny located at 28 2nd Avenue in Paterson, NJ. Joan's residence was an apartment above this bar, and Joan would pull up a stool in the bar at 7:00 am and stay there drinking all day, into the night. Scotch was her drink of choice. The evening of January 11, 1980, Joan was at the bar, where she had been all day. She was drinking with Faye's husband, as she apparently did on a daily basis. All of a sudden Joan started having severe stomach pains. Faye's husband called for his wife to take Joan to the hospital. Joan was admitted, and Faye went back to the bar to close up. She returned to the hospital when a nurse appeared and said, "It will be any time now." Faye looked at her with a confused expression. The nurse said Joan was going to have a baby. Faye said that was impossible, as Joan didn't have a boyfriend. The nurse quipped, "Well, she didn't do it on her own." Joan claimed she had no idea she was pregnant, nor did anyone else. Darlene told me that Faye called her around 1:00 AM to advise her of the situation. My birth certificate states I was born at 1:06 AM. I realized in that instant Darlene had actually been around for my birth. I realized what she was telling me was not fabricated. It was the truth. Up until that moment, I had doubts about what she had been telling me. Partially because the events happened over 30 years ago, and also because I didn't know Darlene at all, I didn't know if she was just making information up as she relayed the stories. I asked her if Joan held me. She said yes, based on what Faye had recounted to her. In that moment, my eyes welled up with tears of sadness, tears of love, and tears of happiness. I finally had the answer I had been wondering about since I was six years old. Joan had held me.

Nostalgia is amazing. I find my strongest nostalgic moments are brought on by smells. I know Joan was a smoker in addition to an alcoholic. I remember as a child I loved the smell of cigarette smoke. I also know as a child, and even now, I find the smell of liquor and/or beer on someone's breath comforting. It makes me wonder, am I experiencing nostalgia from my birth, from when Joan held me against her? Did she smell of cigarette smoke and alcohol? I believe anything is possible, and in my experience, nostalgia always comes from a source, even if that source is unknown.

Darlene reported her family was sworn to secrecy. She told me Joan would talk about my birth every now and again and become nostalgic on my birthday wondering if I was happy and had a good upbringing. Faye would reassure her that she did the right thing. The amazing part is that Faye is the one who contacted the adoption agency. She told Joan she couldn't raise a baby, and the best option would be to put her up for adoption. Tears began to fall after hearing this. Faye knew the life I would've had if Joan had kept me. She knew I needed a stable life, unlike the one Joan had. I always wondered what life would've been like had Joan kept me. I am so thankful that her friends knew enough to place me into an adoption agency, where I would have a chance at being adopted into a family of security and love rather than growing up with a woman who never had a mother, relied on alcohol to get through the day, and didn't know what being a family was like.

Joan drank daily, throughout her entire pregnancy. I was very healthy per the adoption agency's doctor's visit a week after my birth. However, my health quickly declined once I became adopted. I had constant ear infections, and would not eat much until I was around 18 months old. My parents had multiple tests completed on me, including tests for chromosomal abnormalities and Cystic Fibrosis, all which came back negative. The pediatrician diagnosed me as having failure to thrive and possible fetal alcohol syndrome. In the first couple months I did have some features of fetal alcohol syndrome based on the symmetry of my nose and my eyes. The facial features faded away within a couple months, and I eventually gained an appetite. It was thought I did not eat much the first year because of all the antibiotics I was on for ear infections, and the notion of fetal alcohol syndrome disappeared. I was a sweet, shy child who did well in school. As years passed, time would give way to yet another truth. It appears the words of my pediatrician would enter my life once again, many years later.

I asked Darlene about Joan's death. She recalled that Joan was intoxicated the night she died and fell down the stairs as she was headed upstairs to her apartment. I asked who found her. She said her mom had just hired a new bar tender who opened the door to go to work, and Joan fell out of the door, dead. At this point, I sat down on the grass on the bank of the creek. I stared across the creek, listening to the children playing on the other side. Glimpses of shirts and hair and laughter as they chased each other. Full of life, those children had each other. Unlike Joan's life. She appeared to be a loner who never knew her place in life. She went through life intoxicated, never having to feel any emotion. She died alone. I wish she knew that she was thought about every day by her biological daughter, who wished the best for her. My stomach tied itself into knots, and my heart hurt. Nobody should ever live a life like Joan did. I know she made negative choices, and she is responsible for the choices she made. I also know that the circumstances life threw at her were not hers by choice, and those circumstances molded the choices she made.

There were some conversations Darlene and I had that left a smile in my heart. In addition to drinking at the bar Darlene's mom and dad owned, Joan was also an employee. Darlene's mom let Joan open The Copper Penny, tend bar and close the bar. She was considered very trustworthy even though she was constantly consuming alcohol. She told me Joan spent holidays with them; her family took Joan in so she wouldn't be alone. Darlene relayed to me that Joan did smile and laugh on occasion. That statement made me feel better, because it made me realize that Joan did have happy moments. Darlene reminisced how Joan loved her dogs as if they were her own children. I am a dog lover, so I had to ask what kind. Darlene stated Joan loved German Shepherds, and always had at least one as a pet. When she said German Shepherds, I immediately chuckled, because we have a dog named Chester, who is an 8 year old German shepherd mix. They are my favorite dog, always have been. Darlene also chatted about how Joan loved country music, and she would always put on Hank Williams in the juke box. I am a country music lover as well. After she mentioned that, I started to wonder what parts of life do genetics have a hand in? Do genetics play a role in what type of dogs we like, what type of music we listen to? Whether they do or not, I had similarities to my birth mother, and that made me happy. Maybe Joan listened to country music when she was pregnant. Maybe I subconsciously remember the twang of the songs, and that is why I love country so much.

During our phone conversation, Darlene told me how Joan had decided to cut her hair pixie short and dye it red. Within the last week I had chopped my hair off to a pixie cut and had it dyed a reddish black to cover the white. I think if Joan and I had stood across from one another, we could be each other's reflection. I asked Darlene if her family had any photos of Joan, and she said all the family photos were in a shed of her mom's that had weathered and the photos had been ruined. I thanked Darlene for giving me a visual memory of Joan, and for leaving me with the knowledge that she was "not a bad person," as she quoted. I thanked her for giving me peace knowing Joan had people who took her in as family, and knowing I was held by her and thought about. My soul was feeling pieced together after so many years of being frayed. Darlene and I said our goodbyes, and I walked into the house feeling serene and at peace. In the weeks that followed, Darlene saw a photo of me in a cowboy hat. She commented on the photo, writing that my smile and my big dark eyes were identical to

Joan's. I was finally hearing what I had longed to hear for

so many years. "You look like her." Those words were

now permanently etched on my heart and in my soul.

Chapter Eleven

Memories Unlocked

Joanie at her "home"

As I entered the house, my mouth alternated from a smile one second to a look of deep thought the next. My husband caught the look on my face, and asked what was going on. I looked up at him, and told him I had just spoken to the daughter of the bar owner of the bar Joan worked at before she passed away. He inquisitively looked at me, and then asked what she had said. I relayed the conversation to him, and told him I felt a weight lifted off my shoulders. I told him I felt that maybe The Inquisition was complete and Joan's file could finally be laid to rest.

I would say about 14 days passed, if even. I thought the information Darlene imparted would've been sufficient to fill that void in me and to give me eternal peace. It wasn't. I google mapped Joan's apartment. I then maneuvered the cursor so the door she fell out of was showing. Yes, this is a bit morbid and creepy for lack of a better word. Why did I do this? I wanted to try to place myself where Joan had lived, where she had taken her last breath. It is odd, but it made me feel at peace. I had this desire to go to this apartment complex. The bar was no longer there, but the building was. I would like to go to New Jersey and poke around Joan's stomping grounds. I wanted to see in person where she had lived, and where she had died. I also want to eat lunch at the restaurant Mario's my biological grandfather used to frequent in the morning and sometimes for dinner, downing beer and pizza into the wee hours of the morning. The restaurant is still up and running, but under different management. I want a better mental picture of their livelihoods than what I have now. Many probably see my actions as those of a stalker. I understand that, I can see that. I choose to see these desires no different than me taking a trip to see the battlegrounds of the Civil War. They are pieces of American history. Joan's residence and my biological grandfather's favorite restaurant are pieces of my history. History I want to see in person, so I can say I walked in the footsteps and among the memories of my biological mom and grandfather.

I had been speaking to friends about my journey thus far, and how I wanted to know if Joan was indeed intoxicated when she fell. Why did I want to know this? I wanted to know every detail I could to make me understand her life and her death since I was never a part of it. My friends advised me that there should be an autopsy report on file. More paperwork to order? Sure, why not? I opened Joan's file which had not even been put on a shelf yet and took out the Certificate of Death. I searched for the medical examiner's name and the city he worked for. I used the internet and googled his name. I could not find any links to his name or a medical examiner's office. I then scrutinized the certificate of death and found the medical examiner had an address listed on the report. I typed in that address on the internet, and a phone number appeared. I had to take a step back. With only a few clicks and a few number dials, I was going to be able to order Joan's autopsy report. I was going to be able to discover past falls, past fractures, and if she was intoxicated the night she died. I told myself once I had this information, everything would be put away, and I would end my journey. I kept telling myself that repeatedly because I knew even I didn't believe I would be satiated. I dialed the number and spoke to a very pleasant lady. She advised me she had Joan Chanowski's autopsy report and would send it once my money order was received. I went to the bank the following morning, and that afternoon on my lunch break went to the post office to draft up a money order. Once that was completed, I waited for the report.

About two weeks later, I came home from work and went to get the mail. I opened the mailbox and my eyes were drawn to yet another yellow envelope. I pulled it out, and looked at the sender's address: Regional Medical Examiner's Office, Newark, NJ. I started smiling and my heart started pitter pattering. I opened the envelope and slid the report out. I read through each page, placing my finger under each word so as not to miss any of them. This is what I learned:

1. My birth mother had slightly curly brown hair with gray roots

2. She had partial dentures

3. She shaved her eyebrows

4. She owned a jean jacket and sweat pants

5. She wore jewelry

6. Evidence of old injuries over the backs of both hands, right knee and left elbow

7. Her blood alcohol content was 3 times the legal limit in New York

8. Paramedics had attempted to resuscitate her to no avail

9. She dislocated the first vertebrae of her neck attached to her skull when she fell down the stairs, causing her death

10. She had blunt trauma to the head as evidenced in the 4 inch hematoma on the back of her head

11. The lady that identified her was "the decedent's friend, Flora."

I started laughing. I couldn't help it. Shaved eyebrows? Very strange. I reread a few times the clothing and jewelry

Joan had on when she arrived at the morgue. I now had a vision of Joan in my head, and her clothing and jewelry reminded me of the way I have dressed at times. Casual and comfortable. I felt a connection to Joan right then, a connection a mother and daughter may feel when they look at one another when out on the town, and realize they are dressed similar. I continued to read the report, and I read that they had attempted to revive Joan. I started to wonder if she had been lying there alone for a while. I wanted to know how long, the certificate of death did not say. I wanted to know if she almost survived. These are questions I would not pursue. I decided not to attempt to find out if Joan almost survived, because then I would ruminate over the fact that she could've lived had she been found earlier. I would've been opening a whole other chapter in my life that I was not ready to face. I stared at Flora's name. She was Joan's friend? Darlene had not mentioned Joan having any friends. She had mentioned that the lady who found Joan had just started bar tending for her mother and she could not remember her name. I decided in that moment my journey was not yet complete because now I was going to begin a search for Joan's friendship with Flora and how deep it actually went.

I searched on 411. Com, and produced an address for Flora, but no phone number. I compiled a letter to send to her, but then I let it sit on my desk for a couple days. I debated about mailing it once it was written. This is the lady that found Joan after she had died. What feelings was I about to conjure up for her? I decided I would send the letter out and wait to see what transpired.

June 24, 2013

Dear   ,

My name is Rebecca Tillou. My maiden name is
Rebecca Kulak. What I am about to tell you will probably
appear strange to you, and I am sure you will have
questions. I was born on January 12, 1980 in Bergen
County, NJ. I believe I was born at Valley Hospital, as my
birth certificate states I was born in Ridgewood, NJ. I was
placed for adoption through an adoption agency by my
birth mom, JOAN CHANOWSKI. She got pregnant with
me when she was 39 years old. I have a copy of her will
that she had Faye write for her in 1992, and then Faye and
her daughter Darlene signed it. I have been in touch with
Darlene, and she has given me information on my birth
mom Joan, and her life. How did I get your name? It is on
Joan's autopsy report. It has you as the decedent's friend
who identified her…I apologize if I am bringing up
horrible memories. I was told by Darlene that you worked
at The Copper Penny with Joan before she passed.

What am I looking for? I want to speak to people who knew Joan and maybe have photos of her. Her decision to place me up for adoption was an amazing choice. This journey for me is almost complete; the last thing I desire is to speak to people who knew her up until she passed on. All I am asking for are memories of her spirit, smile, and attitude. Even if the only memories I have are told to me by someone else, I will take them. Any help you could give me, I would appreciate it. I have lived an amazing life, am happily married with two sweet little boys. Below is my contact information. I know you do not know me, and are probably hesitant to contact me, but I am hoping you will, and help me complete this Journey I have been on. Thank you for your time.

Two weeks after I sent the letter, my husband handed over an envelope with a hand written address from Flora:

July 7, 2013

Dear Rebecca,

I received your letter, and was shocked to learn that Joan had a daughter, I was not real close to Joan, we were co-workers at the Copper Penny.

I know Joan had a black German Shepherd that she loved and she lived above the Copper Penny. As I said before we were co-workers not really friends, when I came to work Joan would go home.

Your letter brought up memories from that night that I haven't thought about in years. Joan's dog (I'm sorry I don't remember the name) was the reason I went to the door. The dog was outside crying which I knew something was wrong, because I know she loved it and never left the dog alone. I went to take the dog inside and that is how I found Joan. I then called 911 then Faye, when Faye came she took over.

I have been in contact with people in New Jersey asking them if they had photos or anything of Joan's and they say no. If anything does come to me I will keep your address and send them to you.

I am sorry I am not more help

Sincerely,

I read Flora's letter a couple times, and while reading the letter I felt twinges of guilt but at the same time I felt blessed. I felt guilty that my letter had ignited in Flora disturbing memories after years of those memories being laden down by other memories, probably happy ones. I felt blessed that although I conjured up less than pleasant memories for Flora, she still reached out to her friends in New Jersey to see if anybody had memories of Joan to share with me. Flora is an angel, pushing through the unpleasant past in order to possibly bring closure to someone else's unknown past.

I was still yearning to know more about Joan. I wanted to talk to people that knew her in high school. My hope was to finish this search, and at the end have a timeline from Joan's childhood until the day she died. I googled Bogota High School Class of 1958. I came across a class reunion being planned for them in New Jersey the first week of October, 2013. At the bottom of the website was the planner's name, Irene, and her email address. I sent Irene an email and then found her phone number and decided to give her a call. I was hopeful I would be able to hear bits and pieces about Joan's high school days. Irene answered the phone, and I told her about who I was, and my journey searching for my birth mom, Joan Chanowski. I told her Joan graduated with her class. There was silence on the other end, as Irene thought about the name. She told me all she remembered was Joan was tall and quiet. She told me she had an address on Linwood Avenue in Bogota, New Jersey for Joan. I recalled the only address I had for her was on 2nd Avenue in Paterson, NJ. I thanked Irene for her time, but Irene was not ready to end the conversation. She wanted to help. She wanted to find out if any classmates knew Joan, and try to interlock pieces of Joan's past. What transpired in the next two month made me realize there are circles of fate in this world, and I am blessed to have been among a few.

A few hours later, Irene called back to tell me she spoke to her younger sister Jane. Jane told her she would ask her friends from high school if anyone remembered Joan. Irene and Jane were two more angels among my journey to my past. Jane contacted Irene via phone calls and emails. I started receiving emails from Jane. Jane revealed that she had a dear friend named Erin. Erin was her high school friend, and their friendship continued after the high school years. Jane contacted Erin to see if she knew about a Joan Chanowski from Bogota High School. Her response on August 16, 2013 took my breath away. I was not expecting what I saw in the email that followed:

----Original Message-----

From:

To:

Sent: Fri, Aug 16, 2013 8:11 pm

Subject: Fwd: About Joan

I got this from Erin. What a doll!!!Subject: About Joan

Hi, Jane.

Your email gave me the goose bumps when I saw 203 Linwood Avenue and the name Joan! That was right next door to me, and we only had hedges separating our properties. Kitty and Minor Jensen Sr. (the Captain) lived there with their son, Minor J. Jr. (Skipper as I knew him).

My parents were friends with them, and I was friends with
Skipper, who was only a year younger than me and went to
St. Joe's grammar school. He gave me a Captain Midnight
Secret Code ring with labels from Ovaltine, which was so
special to me. We walked to school together all the time
and played together every day. His parents were wonderful
people who took in foster children, the first of whom was
Joan. Since she was older than me, I never really chatted
with her but always looked at her in awe because she was
older, so tall, and had beautiful brunette hair in a ponytail.
I still remember her always wearing her Bogota jacket.
She was quiet, reserved and always respectful, but
sometimes walked slumped over and looked sad. We
always said hello to one another across the hedges. I never
knew she had a child--in the 50s, no one would tell you that
in those days. After her, there was another foster child
named Sally and then one closer to my age, actually
younger than me, named Jimmy, who had been beaten by

his mother. His nose was broken, and he told me she banged his head on the bathtub faucet. I remember feeling for all of them, but I knew "The Captain" and his wife would do a good job with them. We never saw any trouble over there, and their biological son, Skipper, was such a good kid.

The last time I saw Skipper was in 1984 at my aunt's funeral. Later on, I had coffee with his mother and the Estonian neighbor, Mrs. Dreyman, who lived to their left, at my house when I lived in Paramus. I heard that Skipper's mom had passed away since then and that he lived at 203 for a while and got divorced. I knew his dad had already passed several years before that. I had heard, maybe mistakenly, that Minor J. Jensen, Jr.--Skipper--had moved to California after selling 203, but I just looked on People Search and see he may be in North Carolina.

I had tears in my eyes hearing that Joan was dead because there was a connection, maybe a little "hero worship", and sad that her child could never meet her. Perhaps Skipper is on Facebook or something because he is the one that could tell her child what a nice person she was. He lived with her like sister and brother.

Well, I'm glad the reunion is moving along, and I'm happy that you thought you had more fun doing it with me because I feel the same about you! We had a great time! I hope we do have a Sunday meeting with you, Marie and Linda in Paramus soon. I always look forward to seeing you.

Yes, all is okay with me. Still busy with the family and "watching over" everyone. Somehow, I think that is my job! Hope all is ok with you and hope to see you soon. I really wish Joan's daughter could make a connection with Skipper; he could tell her so much! I miss Skipper, and where the hell is my Secret Code Ring? (Only in the 50s was there a Skipper.)

Talk about fate! The fact that I chose to contact Irene, only because she was the head of the reunion! Through her, I was introduced to Erin. Erin not only knew of Joan, but lived next door to the foster home that she lived in! Joan was the first foster child in that house! Fate is amazing sometimes. The details Erin remembered were incredible, I could see Joan so clearly. I became sad as I read about her appearing sad at times and walking slumped over, as if she was conscious of her height. I feel for Joan and the life she had, it seems like maybe she never knew her place in this world. Erin thought so highly of Joan, she had said there was an element of "hero worship." If only those positive thoughts could've transcended into Joan's beliefs about herself.

The foster family she stayed with on Linwood Avenue was stability for Joan in her high school years. Years where stability is important as one tries to figure out what to do and enters into a world sometimes teemed with uncertainty. I did attempt to contact Skipper in August of 2013, and I believe I got in touch with his son, who returned my phone call, and left me a message. I did not attempt to contact him until January of 2014. I hadn't felt the urge to try to connect with him after Erin's emails, as they were so vivid and realistic. I didn't feel as empty after reading Erin's emails. In January 13, 2014, I had been typing this book, and I decided if I could connect with Skipper's son, who could lead me to Skipper, then I would have more stories to learn and more stories to tell. I called Skipper's son Chris, and left a message. I then used 411.com (White Pages, 1998-2014) reverse phone search and learned his number was a cell number. I figured I would try to text him to let him know I was not a crazy lady soliciting random useless information. He returned my text and wrote to call him at 3:00 pm. I had a meeting at 3:00 pm that day, so no call was ever made. I texted him a couple more times, explaining I had sent a letter out to the address I had found. I explained that I was just looking for memories of my birth mother to piece together a vision of her as a young girl. I never received a text message back. I wanted to know the reason why I never received a text back. I figured I scared him away. Or, more than likely he has a family and a life besides filling my memory tree. On February 12, 2014, I decided to try texting Chris one more time. This time he called me, and I let it go to voicemail because I was worried he was calling to tell me to leave him and his family alone. I decided though that I owed him an apology for stalking him. I returned his call, and the man on the other end was sincere and sweet. He told me he was currently working as a police officer tracking down a drug dealer. He then proceeded to tell me that he remembered hearing stories of Joan when he was a little boy, around eleven years of age. He said his grandmother and grandfather were Joan's foster parents, but he doesn't remember details of the stories. He then said his father,

"Skipper" lived near him, and he would have him call me later that same day to discuss any memories he had of Joan. What Chris told me next made my heart drop. He said that the mental state of his father was come and go. He had been diagnosed with a mental illness later on in life, and struggled with it at times. Chris told me he would help me however he could, but he did not know how much his father would remember about living with Joan in his high school days. I ended my conversation with Chris, and my heart was telling me to close this chapter. I chose to not follow through with my contact to Skipper. I didn't want to alter his mental status by having his memory suddenly filled with memories from long ago.

Erin wrote two emails to Jane on August 19, 2013 and August 27, 2013 and painted yet more vivid pictures of Joan. She recalled how in photos I had sent she saw a resemblance between me, my children and Joan. She said Joan was much more attractive than her high school photo.

She also wrote that my hair was the exact color of Joan's. Erin revealed another detailed memory about my birth mother triggered after reading a poem I had written titled, "The Ghost Within." I had written about hair being to her shoulders, and Erin was brought back in time to her and her brother Erik standing in front of a big tree in front of Joan's foster house. Her brother started saying the words, "The Queen of Hearts, she made some farts." Erin told her brother that was disgusting, and she remembers Joan standing with them with light pink lipstick, hair fluffy and around her shoulders, crossing her eyes as Erin's brother made the rhyme. Erin's attention to minute details enabled me to see Joan as if I were standing next to her by that tree. On September 4, 2013 I received an email from Jane. She forwarded yet another email from Erin. It turned out Erin had a friend that lived next door to her back in high school. After hearing about my journey and my desire to know Joan in her younger years, she asked her friend if she remembered her. Her friend replied immediately that she did know Joan and that she was so nice. She used to help her mom clean her house, and she was so surprised she could clean their chandelier without a step stool. After each email I read from Erin, my eyes would become misty, and the corners of my mouth would smile. Everybody had nothing but positive words regarding Joan. Joan's gentle demeanor has been passed on to her daughter, and for that I am forever grateful.

The Bogota High School Reunion for the class of 1958 was held in New Jersey on October 4, 2013. Irene, being the chair of the event, had spoken to a fellow graduate, and she suggested that Irene speak about Joan Chanowski and my journey to finding out who she was. Then she suggested that a notebook and pen be left at the reunion for anyone who may have had memories of Joan. On the night of the event, a notebook was placed at a table by the entrance to the reunion. Irene gave a brief speech about Joan and my search. I received an email the

following day. The notebook was left blank. Irene wrote

to me, stating the few people that did know of Joan

Chanowski only remembered she was tall and quiet. I felt

sad for Joan once again. She just seemed so alone. I felt

blessed to have gotten the details about Joan that I did from

Erin. Irene, Jane and Erin are amazing women, each of

them are angels, and they were my wings that carried me

through a tiny cloud of Joan's younger years.

Chapter Twelve

Onward and Upward

Joan's brother Mark, his wife Nancy, and me:

the first Texas reunion

I spent the next couple months talking on the phone to my biological Uncle Mark, and texting my biological cousins Linda, Karen and Linda's son Andrew. Mark's family were both physically and emotionally close with one another. I would call Mark once a week, and every time I pressed send, I would feel nerves within start surfacing like

I was about to take a big exam. He was not an intimidating man on the phone by any means. He was a gentle man with a Texan accent. Once he started relaying stories of his father and his life growing up, my nerves would calm, and I would close my eyes and try to envision his childhood and my biological grandfather boxing against Joe Louis. Mark is a talker. I would eat up every minute of his verbal reminiscing. After 33 years, I finally knew where I got my talkative gene from. He would sometimes remember a small memory of Joan. One time he recalled how his father had rented a camp for the summer, and he took Mark and Joan with him. Mark remembers he didn't stay through the summer, he stayed a couple weeks, and Joan only stayed one weekend. Mark then returned to his grandmother and Joan to foster care. I felt like with each conversation, Mark's memory was jarred open just a tiny bit, and memories of his lost sister came through. With every memory Mark remembered about his sister, I felt puzzle pieces falling into place in my life that was once full of unknowns and hypotheticals.

I had gone onto Facebook and looked up Andrew Sparks, who is my Cousin Linda's son. From the photos on Facebook, I saw he was blonde, very tall, and handsome. I saw pictures of his daughter Ava, and thought I was looking at my son Nicolas. I couldn't get over the similarities. I understand that for many, seeing people that look like you and your family is nothing special, but for me, it was amazing. To see that my son looked like someone on my side of the family besides his own brother I found mind numbing. I sent Andrew a Facebook message, and within minutes I received a text message from him. From the first text message, we talked like we were brother and sister. He is younger than me by about 7 years. He texted me that his mom Linda was so excited to find out she had a cousin. That smile I had come to know so well throughout this journey returned in this moment. Andrew told me his mom would get in touch with me.

Within a week after I started texting Andrew, I received a phone call from Linda. She is one of the most upbeat positive people I had ever spoken to. Her excitement about me having found her family was so genuine. Linda has a positive outlook on everything, which is similar to me, and her Texas accent makes her that much more enjoyable to speak to. Before our conversation ended, she made it a point to make me understand if she didn't return a text or a phone call, it did not mean she was not thinking about me. It was as if she knew my weaknesses and my fears. She wanted to make sure I knew I was important to her, and she loved me.

About a month after speaking with Linda and Andrew, I received an email from my biological cousin Karen. She sent me photos of her and her 3 sons, and her beloved dog. I asked her for her cell number, and then we began texting. She is another sincere, sweet woman, and I am so happy to have contact with her. I was looking at the photo of her she sent, and we have similar hairstyles, but even beyond that, we have the same nose and eye shape.

Mark has a son Ken, and he and I have been able to connect via email, text messaging and gliding. He is has a great love for the Dallas Cowboys, and is an amazing, strong individual. He has been through incredible hardships and come out of them with a smile. He is a very wise man, and has more than once given me helpful advice on living, friendships, and relationships. He has a great sense of humor, and makes me laugh multiple times a day. I am honored to be in in touch with him, and happy to be able to call him my biological cousin.

After having initial contact with my biological family via technology, of course I had to go the extra step, continue my journey, and go to Texas. Throughout this entire process my husband J had been my rock. He had been by my side every step of the way. He had been quiet through most of it, but always listened when I had news to tell. It had been a difficult journey for Jason at times too. I tend to perseverate over certain ideas, as this book has detailed, and finding out information until I can't find out anything more is a tendency of some with my diagnosis that had not yet been discovered (www.den.org.au).

I broached the subject of travelling to Texas. Jason discussed with me that he knew and appreciated my desire to go and meet my biological roots. We briefly discussed how timing was not good because money was tight. I should've accepted that and waited to travel. Instead, my impulsivity came through full force and I researched flights out of Newark, New Jersey to Dallas, Texas, hopeful for cheap fares. I found flights for one person that weren't outrageous. My reason for travelling sooner rather than later was twofold. The first reason was my impulsive nature, and the second reason was because Joan's brother

Mark was 76 years old and had been through many health hurdles. I wanted to meet him healthy and well. I spoke to my husband and told him I could travel by myself. Jason advised me he knew I would most likely be safe, but there were still those worries and fear of the unknown. He ended the conversation by telling me he knew Rebecca Tillou, and I was going to do what I was going to do. He was right. I wasn't worried at all; the only emotion that was present was excitement in my heart. The next day I discussed dates to travel to Texas with my cousins Linda and Andrew, and booked my flights.

On September 26, 2013, I sat in the Newark, New Jersey airport, waiting to fly into Dallas, Texas to bridge the gene gap. I was going to meet my birth mom's family. I was slightly nervous, but more excited. I felt like it was the first day on a new job. I even set out an outfit to wear, put make up on, and placed gel in my hair.

As I was flying to Texas, I kept thinking, "I am meeting my birth mother's brother." I said to myself," I am meeting the man who is my biological uncle, who got to stay in his home and be raised by his grandmother while his sister was put into an orphanage. I am meeting the man who lost touch with his sister in 1963. I am going to be face to face with the person I broke the news to that his sister had passed away in 1999." It was an event that I never thought I would get to experience. I don't think I ever will be able to express each emotion that was going through my soul at that moment.

I arrived at the airport, and my biological uncle, his wife, and my biological cousin came to pick me up. I was waiting for them curbside, wondering what their vehicle looked like, and wondering if they would drive right by looking for me. I needed not worry. The car pulled up to the sidewalk outside of the airport, and Linda jumped out. I was afraid she may forget to put the car in park she was so excited. My eyes were squinting from the smile on my face. Mark's wife Nancy got out of the rear driver's side door and came around the back side of the vehicle and embraced me. Nancy is an exquisite woman, with twinkling blue eyes and rosy cheeks. She has beautiful white hair, and she wears it cute and short. Linda and I embraced as if we were college buddies reuniting after a summer away from one another. All of the nervous energy I was expecting never surfaced. Mark is wheelchair bound, so he rolled down his window, and I reached right in and hugged him. It was like hugging a longtime friend. Mark is a very tall man at 6 foot 4. He is extremely handsome, with light blue eyes, a manly voice, and a soul full of love. The warmth from each one of them was overwhelming.

We later told each other that the moment we all met, we felt as if we had been friends for years. I never would have guessed that genetics could be so strong when meeting for the first time. I never would have thought an immediate connection to each person was possible, if I had not experienced it myself. It was an amazing feeling, because we had talked on the phone multiple times prior to meeting, but the connection was beyond small talk. It was genetic ties binding our hearts together.

We returned to my biological uncle's house at 11:30 at night, and talked until 3:45 am. Everyone was on an emotional high. When I first entered my uncle's residence, my uncle and cousin turned to each other and said," She looks just like our cousin Karen!" My uncle and I sat down at the round kitchen table in the corner of their kitchen. He turned to me and stroked his chin as he told me, "The eyes, the cheeks, the chin, the smile, you look so much like my cousin, it is eerie." This statement resonated in my heart.

"BAM!" My hands went down on the table as I told a story and my excitement built. A few minutes later, "BAM!" My uncle's hands slammed down on the kitchen table as he told a story. I started to laugh, because it was like watching me in a mirror. I always have windmill arms when I become a storyteller. My uncle is also quite the chatterbox. When I was younger, I was always the last one at the table, because I was always talking. These are minor traits, but they are all a part of the genetic bridge.

While in Texas, I had the opportunity to spend a day with my biological second cousin Andrew, his wife Nina and his 8 month old daughter Ava. It is difficult to express the emotional winds that blew around me the entire time I was in Texas. They were not sad emotions, but excited ones. I went to my Cousin Linda's house two days after I arrived in Texas. I walked in the door and was greeted by a sweet, warm embrace from her. Linda is very tall and thin, and her sense of style reminded me of my mom's style. Very chic and hip. Linda has beautiful reddish hair, beautiful blue eyes, and is always smiling with these perfect pearly white teeth. She is a stunning woman. I stepped into her house, and her husband Jim came over and introduced himself. He was a handsome man with brown hair and big blue eyes, and a southern accent I adored. We embraced as well, and again I waited for the nerves to show themselves, but they never did. I felt as if I was at a friend's house, about to go out for a day on the town. My motions felt so natural. I am now a believer that genetics do tie people together like common bonds tie close friends together, and you feel like you have known those people forever. There are no nerves creating distance. My second cousin Andrew, his wife and daughter came through the door next. Andrew has the Chrzanowski height, coming in at 6 foot 3 inches tall, "and a tad taller," he says. He has blonde hair and blue eyes, and of course, a Texas accent. He was a younger version of his father, from his hair to his distinctive jaw line. Andrew and I were like brother and sister, at least in personality. Physical traits, the exact opposite. He is a burst of constant energy. He is always upbeat, and loves to laugh. He is a male version of me. His fiancée Nina is a gorgeous woman, with long dark brown hair, beautiful big brown eyes, and a great sense of humor. She and I got along like girlfriends should. We talked, we laughed, and we had a good time. I was excited to meet each one of them in person. The day started out with all of us doing a shot of Tequila. Everyone was happy and carefree, and I loved it. We then headed out to a brewery. It was an awesome first date! I felt so much happiness emanating from each of them that day. I was in my element, as were each of them. We were standing in line, waiting to enter the brewery, and Linda and I were chatting about baby Ava. She said she loved her granddaughter to pieces, and she was pretty much a very happy baby, except she could get a little cranky when she was tired, and she would rub her ears. I had Linda back up and restate those last words. In front of my eyes, I saw the word, "Genetics!" pass by. Ava and I had a quirk in common! Ear rubbing must be a Chrzanowski trait!

There was never a quiet moment in the conversation. We got to chat about what each family did for their holiday traditions, and both families love to watch The Christmas Story and Christmas Vacation over the Christmas holiday. We talked about the rest of my family meeting their family one day, and I am hopeful that moment will come. Two families separated by circumstances and brought together by fate. The day ended with a big family dinner with my biological cousins, their children, and my biological uncle and his wife. It was a great dinner at an amazing outside Mexican restaurant. I know the whole family rarely gets together due to work schedules and life, so I felt blessed that I got to be with the whole family at once (well, almost whole, Kenny was not there, and I missed meeting him). It is interesting how one event, like a girl finding her birth family, can bring a family together, if only for one night.

At the reunion dinner, I got to meet Karen, her son Kyle and his wife Heather. Karen is very quiet, tall, thin, and she has a short blonde hairstyle that I admired and wanted to emulate. She has these intense blue eyes I loved, and a lovely smile. Another beautiful Chrzanowski.

Heather and Kyle were newly married, and they were both very kind, ambitious individuals. Heather has this amazing thick, blonde hair I adored, and beautiful facial features and complexion. Kyle is a very handsome man, with black hair and cut facial features. Both of them are very attractive. I wished I could've spent more time with them getting to know them. Karen, Linda, Mark and I all had the Chrzanowski nose, and that was about it. If you stood all of us next to one another, one would probably never put me as a Chrzanowski, but it was more than just physical traits. There were similar personality traits between each of us, and there was an unspoken genetic bond that all of us felt. It was indescribable, and indisputable. It was an amazing reunion. I felt like I belonged, I never felt like an outsider.

The next day my cousin Linda, her husband Jim, Andrew, his daughter Ava and I went to a Texas Rangers game. That night, I got the opportunity to hang with Linda and Jim by ourselves. We had some wine, chatted, and they made a delicious dinner. It was nice to have an intimate dinner with them and get to know them without multiple conversations going on around us. We were seated at dinner, and Jim said he was watching me walk earlier in the day and said to himself, "That walk is definitely a Chrzanowski walk." I was elated. I have never been given so many statements about how I look or act like someone. I loved every minute of it. I ended my trip to Texas by spending time with my biological uncle Mark and his wife. We went into Dallas and I learned about John F Kennedy's assassination. Mark is an amazing man, full of knowledge, and with such a positive outlook on life. He enjoys history, and has lived through so many important events. His wife is incredible also. She and I are very similar in that we are easy going, we enjoy lounging around in comfortable clothes, and we love to laugh. My uncle, his wife and I were sitting around the kitchen table before I left. My uncle's wife explained how their son Kenny wrote poetry when he was younger. I stared at her, because I have written poetry since elementary school. I have always loved to express my emotions on paper, a characteristic that the origin of I had always pondered, and now I had an answer. This was a night for memories to flow. My uncle, aunt and I were sitting around their kitchen table. My uncle was sipping on a beer, and my aunt and I had opened a large bottle of white wine. Earlier in the day, my uncle had taken out photos that spanned many years. We sat there, enjoying each other's company, sipping our drinks, as my uncle recounted the story that went with each photograph. He had four albums, and a little paper bag with old photos in it. The photographs he first showed me were of my biological grandmother and grandfather before they had any children. I saw Mark's features in both of his parents. I saw Joan's slender build in her mother. There were also photos of my biological grandfather in front of an old fire truck. Again, I saw similarities between Mark and his father. With each photo that he showed me, I got glimpses of the Chrzanowski family genes. I did not see myself in any of the photos, but I did glimpse Dominic's height and dark hair through my biological grandfather. The next photos Mark showed me were of him as a young man, right out of the military. I took the photograph of his father and put it next to the photo of him. The similarities were uncanny. They were both attractive, strapping young men.

We went through each photo in detail. He is like me in that he loves looking at photos of the past. He loved reminiscing about the stories that went with the photos. With each page that turned, I would search for a photo of

Joan and him. There were not any. Many of the photos were of my aunt and uncle in their younger years, when my cousins were toddlers and young children. I can remember sitting in that kitchen chair, and studying the faces of my cousins when they were younger. I was searching for similarities to me. I didn't see any, except for our nose. The only one that I looked similar to was Joan, and my uncle's cousin. I have to be honest. After going through the photo albums, and not seeing anyone that resembled me, I started to doubt if Joan had the same father as Mark. My memory slid backward to the first time I spoke to Mark. He had said his mom gave birth to him and then up and left when he was ten months old. Then his father went to New York and met up with his mom again, and she got pregnant with Joan. Joan was born and she left again. She never came back. Joan went into an orphanage, but Mark does not know why. Mark was only a little boy when Joan left the house. I started thinking maybe my biological grandfather was not Joan's father. I spoke to Mark after I returned from Texas, and asked if maybe his father was not Joan's father. I wondered because I didn't see any similarities between Mark's family and me, and also because Joan was placed in an orphanage. I thought maybe the family suspected Joan was not my biological grandfather's daughter, and therefore Mark's father and grandmother did not want to raise her. Mark said his father was her father, he was sure of it. I never asked the question again. I do have an article about my biological grandfather. He was inducted into the Bloomfield High School Hall of Fame in 1983 for boxing, in Bloomfield, New Jersey. The article discusses his boxing career, who his wife was, and states he had two children, Mark and Joan. I read this article a few times, and that statement made me believe once again that Joan was my biological grandfather's daughter.

Mark and his family are my biological family, and I am blessed they have let me into their family circle with open arms. It is just hard when there are unanswered questions, and they are questions that will never be answered with certainty. This family opened their homes and their hearts to me. After my trip to Texas, my genetic puzzle was complete. I had been blessed with yet another amazing chapter in my life.

Chapter Thirteen

The Road Continues

I returned from Texas and placed Joan's file on the bookshelf in the computer room. I felt complete. That void in my heart, my soul, and my life had finally been filled. It was time to focus on the here and now. It was time to focus on my amazing boys and incredible husband.

The last week of October 2013 I was leaving a two hour meeting at work. I looked down at my phone, and I saw I had a Facebook message from an unknown person. I started to read it, and it was from a lady named Dotty who grew up with Joan. I had just put Joan and my journey to rest. I had finally felt I could take a deep breath and exhale. Then I started reading this message:

Hi Rebecca, My name is Dotty. I am writing with

information regarding your birth Mom, Joan Chanowski.

My Dad, who is deceased, owned taverns in NJ when I was

a kid. (I am 56 years old) Joanie worked for my mom and dad for about 10 years or so as a barmaid. First at the Manor club on railroad ave in Paterson and then at the Hillcrest Tavern on union blvd in the Totowa section of Paterson. This was In the 1960s. My dad bought a tavern in Passaic in early 70s and she did not work for us after that. She stayed In the Totowa/paterson area and we lost track of her. Last my mom knew she was working at a bar called the Copper Penny also on Union Blvd. This was early to mid 70's. As far as I know she never learned to drive. My parents used to drive her and she would visit and hang out with us very often at our house. She grew up in an orphanage and I know she had a brother but I don't think she kept in touch with him. I have very fond memories of Joanie and always wondered what happened to her and every once in a while I would "google" her name and last time I did your name came up and I discovered she had a daughter. I spoke to my mom and she gave me some more info. I am hoping we can find a picture of Joanie for you.

She also had a baby boy around 1970 when she was

working for my parents and he, like you was given up for

adoption. My Mother is not sure of the date or exact year

but she said he was born at Paterson general hospital. I

remember it was in the summer because she recovered

from giving birth at our house and I was old enough to

somewhat understand what was going on. My mom

remembers he was adopted out immediately and that the

adoptive parents name began with a C. Anyway back to

Joanie.....she loved horses and German Shepherd dogs..

She had a German shepherd named Smokey when she lived

in a apartment above my Dad's bar. She loved to go

swimming with me and helped me do paint by numbers. We

painted horses on black velvet. I remember my parents

dropping me and my little sister and Joanie off at the movie

theater In Clifton to see Mary Poppins which probably

would be 1964. I will always remember that because it was

the first time I saw a movie in a theater. My Mom also remembers she worked for the phone company before she worked as a barmaid and she had a friend named Jane Massey and they would come to the bar for drinks and that is how she ended up working for my Dad. I hope this helps you. If you have any other info about Joanie please let me know. Somehow I guess she ended up in Bergen County where you were born. Sincerely, Dotty

Chapter Fourteen

Others

Dotty and her sister playing checkers with Joanie, circa 1967 (my first photo of Joanie)

I became speechless as I came to the following part: "Your birth mother had a baby boy in the 1970s and gave him up for adoption." I must have turned white...I became weak in my legs. I could not concentrate the rest of the day at work. My mind was spinning. All these years, I had always wondered if there were others, because she had me at 40. The adoption agency told me they did not think there were other children. Joan's file would be reopened that night. I kept telling myself I had learned from my journey of finding Joan and her family. I would not become consumed. I realize now that is not an easy rule to follow. There are many families out there that know their roots, from where they grew. Now I do too, but finding out I have a biological sibling out there somewhere, it made me want to water my curiosity with an investigation, so I could hopefully attach my biological roots to each other.

I went home that night, and sat down with my husband. I decided this time around, I was going to be up front and absolutely honest about my intentions and feelings. So I told him," I want to find him. I want to find my biological brother" He said he absolutely understood, and then he told me this: I need to slow myself down, and grasp what has just happened. Take it slow; take it one day at a time. So, that is where I was. Taking it one day at a time. For one day only. As one search ended, another began. Thus began my path of perseveration yet again.

The only information I knew is what was written in Dotty's email. I decided to follow the same steps I had when I began the search for Joan. I started by making a list of men with last names that started with C that lived in New Jersey at one time or another. That list totaled around 30. Dotty and I emailed one another after her initial email, and in one email she said she had spoken to her mom, and Dotty's mom told Dotty that the last name Craig kept popping into her mind. I was ecstatic when I received this piece of information. I came up with a list of 8 men with the last name Craig who lived in the state of New Jersey at some point in their life. I had addresses for them, and sent out letters explaining who I was and that by the way they had a sister. I had gotten in contact with a few of their wives, and they had been sweet and supportive, but those conversations had ended with names being crossed off. I received an email from a wife of one man, and she was so amazed at how determined I was. She and her husband wished me the best of luck. After I received this email, I put the rest of the names aside. As I learned when searching for Joan, "You can't know what you don't know." Choosing to search for my biological brother was a bit more complicated than searching for Joan in that I knew Joan knew about me. She carried me for nine months, she gave birth to me, and I at times crossed her mind. I was not sure if my biological brother knew he was adopted, and if he did know, was he in a position to be open about a biological sister coming into his life? I had to tread a little lighter on this search. So, Joan's file was put away on the bookshelf once again. If one of the Craig's' I did contact was my biological brother, and he reached out, then a new chapter in my life would begin. If none of the men I sent

letters to shared genes with me that was ok. Eighteen

months after receiving information about having a

biological sibling, the search ended. I had diligently

searched off and on. My last searching efforts included

www.Classmates.com, www.veromi.net, which was a site

to search for dates of birth and possible relatives, and

Facebook. I came across a man who had a birthday in the

parameters I was searching for. I searched his possible

relatives and reached out on Facebook to the one lady that

came up. I received a response back, and the lady said her

husband was adopted, and everything I had sent her added

up except he was not born at Paterson General Hospital, but

at St. Mary's. She told me her husband was a private

person who did not discuss his adoption much, and had no

desire to search. She told me I could contact him on

Facebook, and gave me his alias. Before I sent him a

message I reached out to Dottie to converse with her mom

about the hospital my biological brother was born in. She had a conversation and responded that her mother now said it was not Paterson General but a different hospital. She was adamant it was not St. Mary's. Dottie finds this strange, because her and her siblings were all born at St. Mary's. After Dottie relayed that information to me, I also found it strange that Joanie's son would not be born at the same hospital, since she was part of Dottie's family for a while. I decided I had nothing to lose, and I sent this prospective biological brother a message, with all of the information I had been given by Dottie. He wrote back saying he was not my brother. I proceeded to write him that I can respect his opinion, but if he ever changes his mind, there is medical history to be aware of. I proceeded to write about diabetes and heart disease in the Chanowski men. He responded with a thumbs up icon, and that was that. His Facebook profile is very private, but I was able to get two photos of him. One was shooting a gun at a range, and another was him and his wife. He looked NOTHING like me. I was able to blow up the photo of him and his wife, and Dottie and I both agreed, his eyes resembled Joanie's. That was it. No other similarities. I was scrutinizing the photo of him at the gun range, and I noticed he was shooting left handed. I Facebook messaged his wife to ask if her husband was left handed. She responded, "Yes." She then wrote that her husband wanted her to cease conversation with me, and although I could tell she wanted to continue our conversations, and see if we are related, she had to respect her husband. I wrote her back that I completely understood. I have not spoken to either of them since. I do think I found my biological brother. Dottie and I think my brother was born at St. Mary's, and her mom is mistaken. His eyes resemble Joan's in shape and color, he was born in the right time frame, oh…and he is left handed. So am I.

In the email Dotty had sent me, she had written memories that came to her about swimming with Joan in the summer months and painting horses on black velvet. My mind reeled back to my birth mom's sheet of non-identifying information. "Hobbies: swimming and horseback riding." When I first discovered who my birth mom was, and talked with Darlene, the bar owner's daughter, I asked her about swimming and horseback riding. She said she had never heard about Joan doing those things. So, after that, I thought my birth mom had put down things she wished she could have done, or maybe things she had hoped I would take an interest in.

It turns out my birth mom formed a special bond with Dotty. I know this because my birth mom chose to write down the two activities she did with Dotty on a form she had to fill out to give her daughter up for adoption. Before talking to Dotty about my birth mother and brother, I was very sad, because I thought my birth mother had led an extremely dark, sad life. Based on the stories told to me by Darlene, my birth mother could not do anything on her own, except take care of a bar. She couldn't even take care of herself. Dotty was astonished to hear how Darlene described Joan, and proceeded to paint another picture. A picture that proves my birth mother had days filled with joy and laughter as well. Now, her days of happiness were when she was younger, but at least her life was not totally immersed in sadness.

I learned my birth mom played the role of a big sister, and a fun one at times. Dotty remembers my birth mom went with her to her first movie in a movie theater, *Mary Poppins*. She remembers my birth mom loved buying and wearing nice jewelry, a trait that I inherited. Dotty recalled that her mom, who was like a mom to Joan, remembered how Joan was soft spoken, but she also had an edgy side to her. This side would come out while bar tending if needed. It reminds me of how I can go from zero to sixty in a flash, most of the time at work when dealing with customers. Now, mine is a by-product of a choice Joanie made when pregnant. Joanie's was…well, I am not sure. It is most likely just environmental and how she had to fend for herself most of her life. She had to grow up pretty quickly. If she didn't stand up for herself when she needed to, who would? Or, maybe it was the scrappiness of her father she inherited. Dotty remembers Joan loved German Shepherds, as do I. My birth mom made an impression in Dotty's life, and a positive one at that. Dotty revealed to me that she had a few good memories of her younger years, and many of those memories included Joan. It seems Dotty and I were both searching for my birth mom throughout the years, and although my birth mom has passed on, Dotty and I connected. Through our connection, I learned about my birth mom in her 20s and 30s, and Dotty reminisced about a woman that she once knew, loved and cared for. It was a win for both of us.

After receiving that first Facebook message from Dotty, I messaged her back, and exclaimed how excited, nervous, and shocked I was to read her message. I received an email from Dotty a week after we started emailing one another. It had an attachment. I opened the attachment, and my smile became painted on my face. In front of me was a photo of Joan. It was a profile photo, taken around 1967. She was playing checkers with Dotty and Dotty's sister at their house. That photo was my profile. Exactly. It was also somewhat similar to my biological Cousin Linda's profile. I started to cry. I had pretty much given up on ever getting photos of Joan, besides the high school yearbook photo that did not even do Joan's beauty justice according to Erin. I stared at that photo. She looked so serious. A couple weeks later Dotty sent me another photo of Joan. It was blurry, but I could make out the facial features which were identical to mine. She was wearing a wig, and Dotty informed me that Joan had short hair and wore wigs when she worked at the bar. The photo was taken in the early 1970s, and she was with her German Shepherd Shawn. I hold onto these photos and giggle every time I peek at them. I believe everyone comes into your life for a reason, and Dotty and her mom had come into my life to give me visions of Joan as a young woman before she fell away from happiness. My desires were finally fulfilled. I believe I came into Dotty and her mom's lives to let them relive the happy moments of the past, and smile as more memories were unlocked. A couple years later I would receive a Facebook message from Dotty's brother, stating that he had a photo album of Joanie's that he had found while cleaning. He had received items his father had when he passed away, and this album must have been one of them. His father was Joanie's boss when she worked at The Hillcrest Tavern. He told me he would take the photos out of the album and send them to me. I received the photos about a week later, and there were about 20 of them. All but two were taken at the bar where she worked. The other two were of Joanie with horses. The photos captured Joanie's two favorite pastimes. Drinking and horseback riding. Each photo of her could have been me, we looked so similar in each one. I felt elated to now have these photos in my possession.

On January 11, 2014 around 9:00 at night, the night before my birthday of all nights, I received an email from Dotty. I had emailed her the night before, because I had been thinking about her and her mom and how I had not heard from Dotty in about a week. In the back of my mind I was worried I had said something at some point to offend her or her mom. I couldn't think what I could've said, but I was fearful just the same. The email I received from Dotty created another twist in this adoption journey. Her mom had told Dotty that Joan had said a guy named Richie was the father of the baby boy, but Dotty's mom knew better. Apparently, Joan had dated a man named Richie way back when, but had not seen him for years. This email was full of information that made my mouth hang open and my fingers drop on the keys, scrolling random letters across the screen. Joan had put on my non-identifying information sheet that my father's name was Richard. Dotty and I have both concluded that Richard was a ghost name. There was no Richard when she got pregnant with me, and no Richard when she had her son. It was a name she pulled out to write on the piece of paper before handing over her children for adoption. Why would she not put the real father's name down? Well, either because she didn't want to bring the real father into the ordeal, she didn't know who the real father was, or, and this is what Dotty and I believe, my father was someone who frequented The Copper Penny, and my biological brother's father was someone who frequented The Hillcrest Tavern, where she worked with

Dotty's family. Our fathers were men that would sit and drink every night with Joan. This would make sense. It would explain why Joan's pregnancies were a secret, and nobody spoke about them after the babies were born. The only people that knew were Joan and the owners of the two bars.

Dotty and her mother are strong, incredible women. The last words Dotty put in that email on January 11, 2014 were, "You are very blessed that Joan did not drag you down with her and you were given great parents!!!" I am blessed, I will never question that. I am amazed at how fate comes into our lives when we are not asking for it, but we welcome it without any doubts. I discovered through Dotty that I have a biological brother, and that my father was most likely not named Richard. Dotty was brought into my life to shed happy memories and photos of Joan.

On January 12, 2014, I turned 34 years old. It was a different birthday than the thirty three that had past. I looked at my birthday in a whole new way. I now had my history. I knew who my birth mom was. I had engaged in conversations since May of 2012 that painted a picture of Joan. I knew of her struggles, I knew that she was a caring, generous individual who was an orphan and didn't know her place in this world. The most important factor to me when I celebrated my birthday in 2014 was that I knew Joan had held me when I was born. When I turned 34 years old, I celebrated the circle of love that had been created. The circle made up of genetics and angels. This is the first birthday I had been able to give thanks to my birth mother using her full name. "Thank you Joan Chanowski for choosing life for me." I know for many this simple thanks is silly and meaningless, but to me it means so much. I now can put a face to the lady who gave birth to me.

Today I am able to thank her for giving me up for adoption instead of keeping me just so she wouldn't be lonely anymore, and just so she could feel loved by a family member. I now have Joan Chanowski's story to tell on my birthday. Some may have viewed Joanie as no good and weak for giving her child up, but to me, she is one of the strongest women I have ever come to know.

I had sent thank you cards to Dotty and her mom with personalized messages in both. I placed photos of me and my boys in Dotty's mom's letter. I wanted to make sure they knew how much I appreciated them opening their memory boxes and their hearts to me. I received a letter back from Dotty's mom, and she wrote that it was uncanny how much I resembled Joan, and that Joan was an extremely hard working, caring and generous person. She said she was a good friend, and looking at my photo and hearing my story brought back fond memories. Here is this lady, 81 years old, holding her arms open to embrace the daughter of a lady who used to be one of her good friends. I was ecstatic when I read how she characterized Joan. Those characteristics are words my family, friends and I use to describe myself. I feel lucky to have inherited such beautiful traits. She was saddened that her and Joan lost touch. Joan had went from working for Dotty's father to working at other bars, and eventually she ended her years at The Copper Penny. Dotty's mom had tried to contact Joan in the 1980's at The Copper Penny, but Joan never returned the phone calls. Nobody knows if she never received them, or if maybe when she moved on at different points in her life, she just left all those that she cared about and those that cared about her to the wind. Maybe Joan operated with an *out of sight, out of mind* mindset. Joan's life had been full of foster homes, and sometimes homes of her father's friends and family who would take her in for short periods of time. I think her mind had an automatic self-protect mode. She had learned not to get emotionally attached to anyone or anything, given she had never been given the opportunity growing up. When she finally was given a couple opportunities with Dotty's family and Darlene's family, her self-protect mode went on and would not shut off. She was most likely scared to become emotionally involved with anyone, because throughout her years she probably would start to trust people and feel at home, and then would be taken away and placed into another family of strangers.

On February 1, 2014, I received a Facebook message from Darlene. All I saw on my laptop was a pop-up that I had a message, and then it gave me a peek at what the message said. I got the feeling she was excited about something, based on the word "excited" that popped into my line of vision. I clicked on the message bubble, and started to read. She wrote that she had found a photo while going through flash drives. She stated she posted a photo to my Facebook page. I fumbled to click on my own page, and there it was. A photo of a group of people emerged onto my screen. There were two women in the back, one dressed in a beautiful navy blue. Then there was a couple in the front. Everyone was smiling. Well, almost everyone. The lady on the right, in the navy blue, had big brown eyes, engulfed with a hint of sadness. Her smile was miniscule. She was tight lipped and her mouth was turned upward very slightly. Everyone else had their teeth showing. Darlene had sent me a photo of Joan with Darlene's mom and another couple they were friends with. Joan was the only one without her teeth showing, a barely there smile coming through her lips. Her eyes had this depth to them, I tried to see into them to the bottom, to see the root of her sadness she seemed to portray. All I saw was a beautiful woman who appeared as if she was a little uncomfortable having her photo taken, like she felt she didn't deserve to be there. I think Joan felt she didn't deserve to be anywhere. The photo of Joan looked less like me than the other two I had. I took my hand and covered up all of her face but her nose and eyes. It was my eyes staring back at me, my eye shape, and my eye color. It was my nose also. I had the weirdest sensation when I looked at just her eyes and nose. It was as if I was looking at one of those optical illusions, and the more I stared, the more I saw my image come through. It was an intense experience for me. Darlene and I discussed the year of the photo. Darlene said it had to be before 1980, because her mom in the photo looked much younger than a photo she showed me of her mom in 1980. It had to be summer, because everyone was in summer attire. We are thinking circa 1975. I am wondering if it was Joan's birthday celebration. Her birthday is August 11, so it is possible. Dotty saw the photo of Joan on my Facebook page, and remarked how beautiful she looked. She looked the way she remembered her, although it was a few years after they had lost touch. She said that Joan didn't look intoxicated, which was exactly one of my first thoughts when I saw the photo. The pose Joan was in took me back to words the dear lady Erin had written about Joan. She had written that she sometime walked slumped over, and appeared sad. That was the image I was looking at. If the photo was taken around the summer months of 1975, that would put Joan at 35 years old. She was one year older than I was in the year 2014. I noticed how tan and smooth and flawless her skin appeared, and how long and skinny her arms were. My skin absorbs the sun the same way Joan's does, and my arms mimic hers in length and slenderness.

One day a couple weeks later, I was admiring how everyone in that one photo looked genuinely happy (except Joanie)…and the man in the photo had my smile–exactly. The same curvature around the mouth, the eyes, the same dimples, the same smile lines! I almost fell out of my chair. How could I have looked and looked at that photo and not even had that thought enter my mind? I immediately messaged Darlene to ask who this man was, and what was his nationality? She told me his name, and told me he was Peruvian. I turned to Facebook, and typed in this man's name. His profile came up. I started sifting through his friends and photos. He is in his late 70s today, and the photos looked much less like me than in his younger years. I found who I assumed was his daughter. I friend requested her, and heard nothing back for about a month. I then decided to request her using a Spanish translator application because I had stalked her page and realized all of her posts are in Spanish. She accepted my friend request within hours. While I was impatiently waiting for my friend request to be accepted, I started googling Peruvian women. In some of the photos, I saw glimpses of my facial characteristics peering at me. I had their complexion, their eye shape, their face shape, and their hair color (before age got a hold of it.) My impulsivity came through again, and I sent the guy's daughter a side by side photos of her father from the bar photo and me. I wrote my conjecture. She responded to me, and wrote she saw similarities, and would talk to her father. She advised me not to say anything to his girlfriend (the same lady from the photo). I responded that I wouldn't, although I had already sent an email to her asking if she knew who my father could be. I then wrote maybe it was her boyfriend. She thought I was joking, although I wasn't. I have not pushed his daughter any further with talking to him about me. He did call me on my birthday in 2015, which I found odd. I also know from his girlfriend that he did know about Joanie's pregnancy with me. That strikes me as odd, but adds to my belief he is my biological father. I do not have concrete proof he is my father, but everyone I have shown the side by side photos to say we look so alike. My mom believes he is my biological father also. Maybe soon I will do a drive by hairing and grab a hairbrush of his to send it to a DNA lab. Until that day, I will sit with my thoughts.

Throughout this journey, many people have commented on my perseverance and how I am blessed to have such a supporting family. Jane, the sister of the coordinator for the Bogota High School Reunion emailed

me on December 26, 2013 and told me I have brought

happiness and hope into her life since sharing my journey

with her. It amazed her to watch my story unfold. There

appeared to be a domino effect, sort of a "pay it forward"

result. As the story effected one person, the change in that

person's life had a positive effect on someone else. I also

felt blessed, because as my biological roots grew so did the

roots to wonderful friendships.

Chapter Fifteen

The Flip Side of the search

When I first decided to search for my birth mom, I was conflicted about telling my parents. I am a people pleaser remember, and I don't like to hurt anyone's feelings, especially my parents. I started the search, and then one day I received a phone call from a Joan I had called earlier in the week. My mom and dad were visiting from South Carolina, and my mom was sitting in our guest bedroom at the time. She saw me quickly leave the living room and heard quick footsteps up the stairs and then heard my bedroom door shut. The conversation I had with the lady ended with a name being crossed off, a dead end yet again. I walked downstairs, and my mom called to me from the other room. "Are you ok, what's wrong?" She then asked who was on the phone, because the way I left the living room, she thought something had happened to someone. I glanced at her, and made the decision to include her on my path to searching for who I was. After I explained my desire to know Joan, her family, and where I came from, my mom looked at me, then looked down at the kitchen table, and her only response was, "Oh, ok." Now, my mother is one of those whose nonverbal cues speak volumes. I knew she was "ok" with the news, but had to digest it. My mom started speaking a few minutes later. She told me she knew why I wanted to know, she was just concerned I would get hurt. She then started asking me about my search process, and giving me suggestions. She said my father had a whole adoption file at home that he would give me to pick through. I just smiled at this statement, because my mom didn't know I was already familiar with the file. She told my father about

my journey, and his sentiments were the same, he

just didn't want me to get hurt. I felt our mother-father-

daughter bond grew in that moment. It felt good to know

they understood, and were in my corner.

My parents came up to visit a month and a half

later, and my dad brought the tattered adoption file folder.

I slowly pulled out each item. There was an envelope, on

which my father had written down the dates for the

progression up to the date the Kulaks went to New Jersey

to get their new baby. I pulled out the sheet of non-

identifying information that I already had, and then I pulled

out this stack of papers with hand written notes with dates

on it. It was a documented timeline of every illness I had

as a baby. My mom was sitting next to me at the kitchen

table. I stared at the packet of paper, and then I gave her an

upwards glance. She looked at me with caring eyes, and

she told me her and my father were so worried about me

when I was a baby. I wouldn't eat the first year of my life, I was constantly sick with ear infections and bronchitis, and I was below the growth chart for height and weight. Her and my father wanted to document every illness and every doctor's appointment. They were terrified of losing another daughter. My mom was fearful that her fears she had before they adopted me were coming true. No prenatal care had taken a turn for the worse.

So fast forward to May of 2013, when I discovered the identity of my birth mom and when I received notice she had passed away. My parents came to breakfast with my husband and our children one day, and both told me they were impressed with what I found when I knew so little. They were floored by my investigative skills and my perseverance. I was pleased, it meant so much to me that they were so proud of me and my accomplishments. I kept my parents in the loop as I found my birth moms family. I later showed my dad a picture of my biological cousin. He reacted by telling me, "You know your birth mom's name, you know she's dead, what else you want to know? I thought you said you were finished searching." I felt like I was a child who had just gotten chastised. I became worried that my biggest fear had become reality. My father no longer approved. I got defensive, and quipped back," Well, I am not done."

I kept going with my search. I went to Texas, I met my biological family, and I still keep in touch with all of them by phone calls or texting. We exchanged Christmas gifts in 2013, and my biological cousin Linda gave me an amazing gift. She created a scrapbook of photos taken when I visited them. She titled it, "My Cousin!" I get chills down my spine whenever I see it. I have come so far. I now know my biological family. On the back of the album, she wrote, "I love you and I am so glad you are a part of my family." I will always cherish this gift. My biological aunt and uncle sent me a Christmas card. There were cute puppies on the front with red bows. On the inside were the following words: *I want you to know, like my children and wife, you have brought so much joy to my life.* Tears lined my eyelashes. This was written by a man with a lot of love, care and respect for family and friends.

He is a very generous, caring, hardworking individual, just like Joan.

My parents come to visit my family in New York every couple months. Throughout my searching journey, my parents would come up, and it would be my mom who would ask about my progress. One night my father and I were discussing my ailments as a baby. We were discussing how when I was a baby I was diagnosed by the pediatrician as failure to thrive. This conversation came up because my 6 month old was sick, and had double ear infections. I told my dad my thoughts about the connection in utero and directly after birth between mothers and children (2003, Verrier), and how I thought that may have been the reason for why I was diagnosed with failure to thrive. He said he doesn't believe that there is a bond in utero or when a baby is first born, because there isn't enough time for a bond to form. I listened to his explanation, and I kept in my mind that he is an individual and entitled to his opinion. I had a copy of The Primal Wound by Nancy Verrier, and before I went to bed that night, I placed the book in my dad's suitcase with a note attached. I wrote that I am a believer of her theory, and I wanted him to take a peek, if for nothing else than to know where my thoughts had originated. I cried after our conversation, because I was hoping he would understand, and believe the theory could be true. I was sad that he had the beliefs he did, but then I thought about the situation at hand, and realized he is not an adoptee, and I am not an adoptive parent. His thoughts are his thoughts, and he has his reasons for them, and I needed to respect them. I was just taken aback because for me to talk to him about my adoption was always a tricky road because I feared my father would think I didn't love him.

A few days after my parents returned home from their visit, I received an email from my father regarding the emotional ties between Joan and me. I was taken aback, His email was the following:

> *You need to forgive yourself, if that's the right way to put it, for being adopted. No one chooses to be born, and no one chooses their parents. Your mother gave you up because there was no way she could take care of you as a single parent. That wasn't your fault. In fact, she did you a huge favor and gave you the chance at a better life than she could provide for you. There was never time for emotional ties, it was NOT a rejection. She was protecting her own survival, and trusted your survival to a caring agency who could find a good home and family for you. You have come a long way*

from there and you should be PROUD of what you
have accomplished when so many people who were
born and raised traditionally have not completed
high school and college, don't have good jobs, or
wonderful happy children.

I read my father's email, and I had different emotions all at once. I was glad he had given thought to my feelings about being adopted. I was intrigued by his opinion on what I considered my birth mother's rejection he considered her protecting her survival. It was an interesting take. I emailed him back, thanking him for taking the time to write out his thoughts and feelings. I realized in that moment that I needed to realize I was lucky to have grown up educated and successful. I *should be* proud of what I have accomplished in life. My father had given me positive aspects in my life that I took for granted. He opened my eyes to how amazing my life is. He is an amazing man and an amazing father. He is a major reason

I have so much positivity in my life. A few days after the emails, I texted my mom to see if my dad had started reading The Primal Wound. She said he had, and he would love to talk to me about what he has read so far. I contacted my father by phone that night. I will always remember the impression he left on me after our conversation. I was nervous when I first started speaking to him, because I have always struggled with deviating from another's beliefs, especially family and close friends. I opened our conversation by telling him I had talked to my mom and she had told me he had started reading *The Primal Wound*. He told me he had, and how it was a very interesting theory. I brought the conversation back to when I was born, and how I had failure to thrive. I discussed with him my thoughts about how it could be the broken bond with Joan. My father said after reading the book, he supposed it could be possible. We had an incredible conversation. I made sure he knew I understood not

221

everyone is going to believe in this theory, I just wanted him to understand where I was coming from. I wanted him to see my adoptee perspective, just as I now saw his adopted father's perspective. This conversation with my dad left me feeling more confident to be open and honest with my father about my emotions towards adoption. One can't grow if they are not nourished with words and ideas. Now, since that conversation, the tables have been turned upside down, and that reasoning in *The Primal Wound* was shaken off, no longer a reason for my failure to thrive. My failure to thrive appears to have been because of a choice my birth mom made day in and day out in the nine months she was pregnant.

Throughout the days and nights of my stroll along my searching path, my mom slowly started asking me how my journey was going. When I got back from Texas, my parents were both intrigued as to how it went. I told them it was an amazing experience, and I was so glad I had the opportunity to go and meet everyone. My biological cousin Linda and my mom are similar in that they are both chic individuals, and have similar decorating tastes when it comes to their homes. I am excited for everyone to meet one day, and for everyone to see the similarities between the Chrzanowski's and myself. As time has passed, my parents have become more accustomed to my search and why I had to do it. I feel more comfortable opening up and telling stories about my trip to Texas, and revealing the character traits of each family member. I still hesitate before engaging in stories with my family about my biological family even though they have accepted that this journey is something I needed to do. I think I will always be a little shy when it comes to these conversations. I never want to make others uncomfortable with my words and actions, especially my family.

Now that my search is complete, I understand my father always supported my search. I now see my father's fears for what they were. He is a father of a woman who has a tendency to become consumed easily in endeavors when they are for her benefit alone, at the expense of family and friends. I started to realize my father may have felt scared by my constant desire to know more. He had seen me stop at nothing to get what I wanted in the past when it came to relationships, and I think he started to have the fear of having to live the nightmare again, only this time my husband and children would be living the nightmare. Looking back at my search, I realize those past tendencies did pop up, but not to the extent they had in the past. My advice to those searching, or contemplating searching, just try to remember your family's feelings. Remember they see your actions inside and out. They are not blinded by desire and hope the way you may be. It is all too easy to get wrapped up in wanting to know, and putting a blind eye to those around you.

My mother's mom, whom to everyone was Granny, did not agree with my desire to search for my birth mother. When I discovered my birth mom's photo on Classmates.com, I posted it on Facebook. I found out later that my cousins were at Granny's apartment one day, and were discussing my Facebook photos of Joanie. Granny may have been elderly, but she heard everything. A couple days after I located Joan, I went to visit Granny with my husband, mom and children. My mom told me to pull up Joan's photo on my phone and ask Granny who it was. "I know who that is, I heard your cousins discussing it." Granny does not mince words, never has. I asked her if she thought we looked alike. She absolutely thought so, and then asked me what I planned on doing next. I could tell in her voice and the look on her face that I should just tell her I was content and let it go. So, that is what I chose to do. My mom revealed to me after Granny had passed away that Granny had told my mom she didn't understand or agree with what I was doing. She felt it was a betrayal to my mother and the entire family. My mom told me not to worry about what she thought. I explained to my mom that not everyone is going to be excited and jump up and down like a frog at the concept of me having found my biological family and having gotten the chance to meet them. I understood that. I told my mom that I admired Granny for her feelings. My mother is Granny's daughter. Granny was a family woman. She would do anything to protect her family. If Granny felt one family member's decisions were threats to another family member, she would listen, but make it known she did not agree. Whether she let her dislike be known by verbal or facial cues, there was never any doubt where she stood. I was Granny's granddaughter, period. She honestly forgot most times I was adopted. She didn't understand why I would want to search for the lady that gave birth to me. In her mind, Joan gave me up, period. Granny did not want my mother to feel slighted or to feel I would forget her and my family and replace them with my birth family. Granny always put her family first. I empathized with her feelings.

There was a post that I received on Facebook during my search. I had been posting the ups and downs of my search journey on Facebook, and I had written, "Tomorrow (January 12) is my birthday, I wonder what my birth mom felt 33 years ago tomorrow." Someone had responded to my post with the following: "You are here, forget her, it's her loss, your gain." I was slightly taken aback when I read the post, but I was not surprised who wrote it. I had a strong feeling that this person did not agree with my search, and I tried my hardest to keep in mind that it is her opinion and she is entitled to it. I am not going to say it didn't hurt, and my initial reaction was to be defensive. I had to take a step back, and when I did, I realized everybody had opinions based on where they stood in the circle of adoption, and although I didn't agree with her statement, I felt I shouldn't become defensive and judgmental. This person has a close connection with the world of adoption, and I wanted to meet with her personally and discuss her beliefs further, to try to gain more of an understanding from where she stood in the circle of adoption. I did get a chance to speak with this woman, and now I know where her fears were born. She is an adoptive mom, and she looked at me with a worried expression as she revealed to me she knew her daughter wanted to search. "But what if she finds her birth mom and forgets about her family?" In this moment, I saw firsthand how fears transcend into adoptive parents minds as well. Her fear came across in her Facebook post as angry, as if my birth mom didn't have a right to know me. Her fear was veiled by strong words. My heart went out to her, and I hope she talks to her daughter about her true feelings and fears about searching. I strongly believe through conversation, two people can bond and doors can be opened.

Chapter Sixteen

Rewind

As many people can probably relate to, my hairdresser is the one person who knows everything about me. So naturally when I started on this journey of finding my birth mom and her family, my hairdresser was given a front row seat on the roller coaster. In a short amount of time, I had spilled my secrets to her. I had only met my hairdresser maybe two months before? I remember telling her when I found out who my birth mom was. She got so excited and hugged me tight. I was taken aback, I think because I hadn't thought it all the way through, I was still in shock mode. I had not let myself take a moment or even days to absorb what I had just discovered. I now had my birth mother's name and a photo. I was still going to that photo of her every 5 minutes and staring at it, amazed that finally I had a reflection staring back at me, and it looked so much like me, but this time it wasn't me! I remember telling my hairdresser that my birth mom had passed away. My hairdresser's smile disappeared, and she got quiet. I continued to tell her I was ok with it, because at least I knew why I was having such trouble getting in touch with her. Then I started wondering if maybe my emotions were all wrong, and then I started feeling guilty inside. I felt like maybe I should feel more emotion towards my birth mom's death.

I told my hairdresser about my biological brother out there among the stars somewhere. I told her how Dotty had grown up with my birth mom and how my birth mom was like a big sister to her. I had been told by Darlene that Joan treated her kids like her own. I indulged my hairdresser with this information as well. Her response surprised me. "I would be so angry at your mom if I were you! She took on other people's children as her own but couldn't keep you." I thought about her statement. I had those same thoughts years ago, when I wondered if Joan had raised other children. Through my search though, as I learned the life Joan had led, I decided anger was not a fair emotion. If Joan had the means to have raised children, she would have, I strongly believe that. Joan treated children the way children should be treated; with respect and care. She was able to handle children for short periods of time, when she was able to give them back for the long term. Watching a child for a day and raising a child are not the same.

Looking back, my emotions during this journey have been different than I and others have expected. I expected to cry hysterically when I found out my birth mom was dead. I expected to faint when I found out I had a brother. I expected to hug my birth family for minutes upon minutes and cry. None of these things happened. I guess my emotions were ones someone may have with something brand new. Something one is not attached to and still learning about. I am ok with my emotions, and in the end, that is all that matters.

Some who knew the struggles and triumphs of my search inquired if I really did feel that my journey searching for Joan was complete, given that she was dead and I was unable to contact her. They felt if they were me, they would still feel a void where Joan should've been. I didn't feel that void. Yes, Joan was no longer in this world, but I had been given glimpses of what her twenties and thirties were like, and also what her forties and fifties were like. I was given a sense of who she was all wrapped up in photos and memories relayed to me over emails, in person, and over the phone. All of these memories filled that void. Did I wish I could've seen her in person, embraced her, and spoken to her? Absolutely. I realized that sometimes in life, Joan's senior superlative was true, "That's the way the cookie crumbles."

In a sense, I did get to meet Joan. When I had been reviewing the death certificate, I searched for a cemetery where she had been buried. It had the name of a cemetery, and then it stated she had been cremated. I thought that was strange, but not having many personal encounters with death, I thought maybe her ashes had been spread at the cemetery. So, I researched the number for the cemetery, contacted them, and asked if Joan's ashes were there so I could go and pay my respects. The cemetery put me in contact with the crematory where Joan's body had been taken. I dialed the crematory, and a young man answered. I divulged who I was looking for and who she was in relation to me. I relayed to him that I knew it was pretty pointless to contact him, because I didn't see why he would still have her ashes. He seemed to want to play along though, and he asked me how long ago she had passed away. I told him fourteen years, and grimaced as I waited for him to laugh and tell me they don't keep ashes from that long ago.   He asked that I give him some time, he will look up her name in their computer and see what he could come up with. About 30 minutes later, my phone vibrated. I answered the call, and the man at the crematory was on the other line. "Um, mam, we still have Joan Chanowski's ashes. I can send them to you if you wish. I just need your address." Fourteen years later, nobody ever claimed them. My stomach turned, my heart dropped, I stammered to have the ashes sent to me. I felt in my heart it was the right thing to do. So, I did get to meet Joan, just not in one piece. I know God had his hand in this turn of events. I was meant to have my birth mother's ashes, because I was the one person preventing her from being at peace, because I wanted to know who she was. Now, I would finally have peace, and she could finally rest.

On June 7, 2013 at 8:30 am, I picked Joan up from the post office where she was waiting. As I stepped out of the car, my legs felt like Jell-O. I closed the car door, and took a deep breath in. I walked slowly and deliberately to the post office door, and pulled it open. My left arm felt like it was doing a bench press, it felt weak with anxiety. The post man pushed a box towards me that read, "*Joan Chanowski's Crematory Remains*. I was not aware of how heavy ashes can be, and I almost dropped the

box as I slid it into my hands. I thanked the postman, and he advised me that I also had a letter returned to me. He took an envelope and put it on the counter. I reached over and put the ashes back on the counter. I picked up the letter and looked at it. It was returned from 28 2nd Avenue, Passaic New Jersey. Joan's address. The coincidence of receiving the letter back the same day I picked up her remains was uncanny to say the least. I placed Joan's ashes in the front seat with me, and drove like a turtle down the roads back to my house in the little town of Voorheesville, NY. I walked gingerly into the house with Joan. I placed the package on the counter, and proceeded to open the edges. Inside was a silver canister, about 6 inches high and 6 inches in diameter. I took it out, and placed it on the counter. The top of the canister was taped down. I opened the top to peer inside. It looked like off white sand. My German shepherd Chester came to sniff her out. Deciding she was ok to be in the house, he retreated back to the couch. I placed the top back on, and texted my husband that Joan was now with me. He asked me if I was ok. I texted back that I was, that I just felt weird. I didn't know what to do with her. I didn't know how I should feel. I didn't know what I felt. It was like I felt nothing, but simultaneously I felt every emotion there is. I went into the guest room and turned on *It's a Wonderful World* by Israel "IZ" Kamakawiwo'ole. I mourned the life and passing of Joan Chanowski. I sobbed, very deep sobs, teardrops falling onto the top of the container. When the song ended, I took a deep breath that shuttered with every emotion I felt for Joan, wiped my tears away, and left the room. It was a bitter sweet moment.

After I mourned Joan's ashes, I just sat, staring at the canister. I didn't know what to do next. Looking back, it was a blessing that I had to go into work later that day. I was not privy to sitting at home, staring at Joan, or what was left of her. I had trouble visualizing that all of those ashes were once Joan Chanowski, a lonely woman who didn't know how to rise above the harsh realities of alcoholism. I kept thinking there were a lot of ashes for one person, but then I thought about what a tall woman she was, as everybody who knew her had stated. I figured it made sense there would be a lot of remains. As I sat, I wished Joan was in front of me, not in a million little sand specs. I wished, for just one day Joan was alive so I may have sat with her and talked. I wished I could've discussed the inner turmoil in her head when she gave birth to my brother and me. I just wanted a physical embrace, a physical connection, if only for a passing moment in time.

When I relay my search journey to others, they always ask what became of the ashes. Originally they were in my cedar closet in the basement, but my mom told me having Joanie in the closet next to where she slept freaked her out a little bit. I told her she had nothing to worry about, if Joanie haunted her, it would only be to join her for a cocktail. I really was not sure what to do with them. I moved her to my bedroom closet, up on top of my lingerie chest. I asked Darlene, the bar owner's daughter if she would like them, since she was like family to Joan. She politely declined. I emailed Dotty and asked if her and her mother would like her ashes, since Joan had been such a big part of their lives, and they are the ones who had made happy memories for Joan, horseback riding and swimming just to name two memories. Both of them also said no and told me I was her daughter who had spent so much time researching who she was. They felt it was only right that I keep them. I asked both families that played roles in Joan's life if they knew of anywhere Joan would've wanted to have her ashes scattered. Darlene said Joan's life revolved around the Copper Penny, and she had happy times there. The bar is no longer there, and I would feel strange standing outside on the corner of 2ⁿᵈ Avenue with a silver canister. Dotty did not have any ideas. I thought about asking if Dotty and her and her mom would want to join me in spreading her ashes. I felt that may have been the way Joan would've wanted it. A family that took her in and a daughter placed for adoption, united together to put her at peace. Then I decided I would spread them by myself. I was going to spread her remains on her birthday, August 11 of 2013, but I could not do it. Her remains are the only physical tie I have of her that I can keep close to me. My friends and family have each told me not to keep wondering when and where to spread Joan's ashes. They have told me I will know when the time is right. During the harsh, bitter cold winter of 2015, as I drove my two year old to his daycare, I passed the same horse farm I pass every single morning. I started to smile, as I glimpsed the beautiful velvet brown horses with their bright purple and pink coats on. I had an idea. Later that day, I contacted that horse farm near my house via email. I relayed my story of search and reunion and asked if I would be allowed to spread Joanie's ashes on the farm. The owner replied back that I would be able to give Joanie peace on her farm. She just wrote I may want to wait until the ground thaws out. I wrote back my thanks, and agreed to wait until spring or early summer to let my mom be free to run like the horses. Well, on March 13, 2016, I travelled to the horse farm, with Joanie once again in my front seat. I pulled into a circular driveway, and in the distance I saw a lady walking towards me, her eyes squinting from the sunshine that was peeping through the clouds, and the slight breeze that was blowing towards her. This lady was the owner of the farm, and the horses. She came up to me, and extended her hand. "Hello, my name is Jean." I took her hand and thanked her for allowing me to give piece to Joanie's broken life. Jean smiled, and it was such a genuine smile, she put me at ease. She asked if she could hitch a ride in my car, and she would steer me to the place I could spread Joan's remains. I started driving down the driveway towards the horse fields. Jean had me veer onto a gravel road and then slowly inch my way through a metal gate, and park in a back field. She had me follow her to a spot covered with newly spread grass seed. "This is where I buried one of my favorite horses." I think this would be the perfect place to put your mom." Now, in my head I had this scenario pretty much playing out the way it had been. I walk slowly over to the burial place, and kneel down over Joan's canister, forgetting I had taped the lid down with layers of scotch tape. I was feverishly trying to open it, because I did not want to take up any more of Jean's time. Finally, I pulled the lid off. I gingerly unraveled the bag with Joanie's remains. I put my hand in for a handful, and my fingers touched solid matter. I pounded the ashes with my fingers. They did not give way. I guess I had not taped the canister air tight. There were some loose pieces, and I managed to spread about three handfuls. Then I placed the lid back on and continued back to my car. I didn't even stop to say some words, or to mourn. I was too embarrassed. I really think Joanie was laughing from up there in Heaven. So, part of Joanie is at peace. The rest of her…well, in a way I let her live out her love of swimming. The first week in April 2016, I took Joanie down the hill in my backyard to the creek below. I again opened the canister, and placed it on the bank of the serene creek below. I had my phone with me, and I searched www.youtube.com for the song *Let Her Go* by Passenger.

I heard the beginning chords of the song, and I reached my hand into the canister and took out a handful of ashes. I threw them into the creek. It was eerie, but in a most beautiful way. I released the rest of Joan's ashes. The last handful was released as the second rendition of *Let Her Go* played its last chord. I know Joanie is at peace now. I gave serenity and peace to my birth mom's once broken and lonely life. My birth mom needs to know that she never was, and never will be forgotten.

Chapter Seventeen

A Look Back

I know some people are probably wondering how I can be 100 percent positive Joan Chanowski was my birth mother. When I finished this journey, there was a little piece of my mind that wondered if she was indeed my birth mother. What if at the finish line of my journey to find Joan, I had found a family and made friendships, but the family belonged to someone else? I emailed the social worker my story. Her reply was all the proof I needed. "Your birth mother would be so proud of you."

Looking back over this long, tumultuous journey that began on January 12, 1980, I realize what an incredible role God and fate played throughout. I remember back to my childhood days, and even days as an adult, before I found Joan Chanowski. I had fantasies about who my birth mother was. I didn't know the truth, so fantasies were my reality, although they were a false sense of reality. I remember when I was getting on a plane with my 4 year old, before I found Joanie, and he shouted, "Mommy look, the pilot looks like you!" I saw the profile, and sure enough it looked like me. I wanted to go up and talk with her when we landed, and use my son as a way of meeting her, telling her he wanted to say hi to our pilot. I had this charade played out in my head. I all of a sudden felt nervous and anxious, because what if she was my long lost relative? The plane ride was riddled with thoughts of the flight attendant being a long lost relative. The plane landed, and it was so hectic getting off the plane, I didn't get a chance to speak to the flight attendant. I didn't want to hold people up behind me because I had some silly vision. We got home, and I googled USAIRWAYS pilots. I found no matches to a Joan. I slowly let that hope slip away.

My deepest fantasy was the need to be held in my birthmother's arms. As a child, almost nightly I envisioned running into her open arms and her holding me tight as she clasped her arms around me. I had fantasies about meeting her and her breaking into tears and saying how sorry she was and how she wanted to be friends. I even had fantasies about my birth father, and him stumbling upon me because he had gone on a search for me after finding out he had a daughter.

I never envisioned my adoption journey to have the twists and turns it did. I never thought Joan would end up on a horse farm and in a creek and that I would not get a chance to speak with her. I certainly never expected to be diagnosed with Fetal Alcohol Syndrome, and my mind to go in reverse to take a look at all of my "quirks."   I have met wonderful people along my path, and through each of them I have learned who my birth mother Joan Chanowski was, and who she was not. I learned that she knew it was a chance giving me up for adoption, because she had been an orphan and a foster child until she was 18 years old. I believe that in her heart, she knew even if I had ended up in the foster system, I would be fed, clothed, educated, and supported by families.   These are all things Joan probably was not sure she could do for me. Joan went through many turbulent times growing up, and throughout her childhood all of her decisions were made for her. She never had much practice making decisions. Yet, when she gave birth to me, she made the hardest, most selfless decision she ever had to make. Joan was a strong woman, and through writing this book I hope I have given her a voice to match her character.

Chapter Eighteen

The "Aha" Moment

Now, throughout my journey I have divulged social issues and personality traits of myself that originally I thought were all due to being adopted. I briefly disclosed that those "quirks" were in fact due to a choice Joan had made while she was pregnant with me. Joan lived the life of a chronic alcoholic. She chose to drink her entire pregnancy with me. The result was a diagnosis of Fetal Alcohol Syndrome at the age of 33. What led me down the path of a diagnosis was a phone call I received from my mom when I was driving home from work one evening in April of 2014. My mom's voice sounded odd, as if she was choking back tears. She relayed to me she had received a pamphlet in the mail that day from the adoption agency she and my dad had adopted me from. She had placed the pamphlet on the kitchen table with the other "mail to be recycled." She was passing by the kitchen table and the letters *FASD* caught her eye. She walked over and took the pamphlet from the recycle pile. She opened it, and read the words, "FASD: Fetal Alcohol Spectrum Disorders." She told me she had an "aha" moment, and decided to call me. Through her tears, she read me the characteristics of Fetal

Alcohol Syndrome, which is listed as a diagnosis under FASD (Bethany Christian Services, 2014). I possess about 90% of the characteristics, if not more. In those moments, my eyes flew open, my mind started reeling with my "quirks" that I had always thought were due to being adopted, but they didn't quite fit into that bucket. I now, in just a couple minutes, was able to explain so much. My impulsive nature blatantly seen throughout my search, my immaturity and my social issues where I divulged private details of my life to strangers and hairdressers. Why I had yelled and screamed at my mom in her kitchen just a couple days before, when she was trying to make sense of my need to know my birth family. Once my mom read me the characteristics, she was not the only one with tears on her cheeks. It all made so much sense.

So, let me take you back to about a week before this phone call took place. I had been visiting my mom and my dad on vacation, and we had just finished dinner. I had followed my mom into the kitchen. We had both had a couple glasses of wine, which helped the words to flow, or rather fly. My mom was trying to understand why I had become so obsessed with searching for my biological family and the essence of *who* each member was. I felt each question as a dart into my brain. My words were quick and loud, like a gun shot. Within two seconds I was yelling and defending, I felt like a coach and a basketball player all at once. The result…was less than ideal. The result was two women yelling, the younger of which was simultaneously crying hysterically. The next morning, I left with my two little boys to head back to good ole' Voorheesville. I saw my mom at Albany airport the day I left her house in South Carolina. She had flown with my older son back to New York on a different flight than me, and then was flying back to South Carolina. She came up to me, and we embraced. We cried, we apologized for the painful words that had been spoken the night before, at that moment not knowing brain damage was to blame. That FASD pamphlet that was placed in my mom's hands a week later gave us both an understanding of my quick biting words. I couldn't take back the way I had acted, but with an explanation, I could now move forward towards controlling my behavior.

"Defined and named in 1973, Fetal Alcohol Syndrome (FAS) is a disorder resulting from prenatal exposure to alcohol. It is characterized by abnormalities in three domains: 1) growth deficiency, 2) central nervous system dysfunction resulting in neurobehavioral disorders, and 3) a specific pattern of facial abnormalities. Confirmed maternal use of alcohol might or might not be documented.

Source: FASD Competency-Based Curriculum Development Guide (2008)

So, what happened next? What entailed after that phone call from my mom? I wanted a diagnosis! I wanted answers. I went to a neurologist after speaking to my primary care physician, who believed I struggled with symptoms of Fetal Alcohol exposure. The neurologist did some neurological tests, and I was unable to perform counting backwards by sevens and struggled naming 4 legged animals. He did some basic research on Fetal Alcohol Spectrum Disorders moments before he saw me, and told me he was not a specialist in it, but did not think I had any physical signs of it. After the testing was complete, he told me I do have mild learning difficulties, and then I had to wait for an appointment with a neuropsychologist for more in-depth testing, which would show exactly where my learning deficits were.

Well, I was referred to two different neuropsychologists, neither one took me. The first one dealt with stroke patients, and the second one I never heard back from. Finally, I decided I would take matters into my own hands, and refer myself to a doctor. Now, what type of doctor? I googled *"Albany, NY Doctors Fetal Alcohol Disorders"* and found the region's only pediatric geneticist (Dr. Natasha Shur*) who specializes in dysmorphology (the branch of clinical genetics concerned with the study of birth defects) and has extensive experience with neurological disorders. All the doctors listed for my Google search were pediatricians and children specialists. I couldn't locate any doctor who diagnosed adults with FASD, so I picked up the phone and called Dr. Shur. I faxed a letter introducing myself, listed all the characteristics I had that I thought may be associated with FASD and provided baby pictures. The office called me back 3 weeks later with an appointment date.

The morning of November 20, 2014 came, and my mom and I arrived 30 minutes early, and walked through a maze of hospital hallways, until we arrived at a Pediatric Genetic Clinic. They were the only specialists in the area that could diagnose Fetal Alcohol Spectrum Disorders. It was as if I had entered Disney World. A huge Theodore Chipmunk stood at the entrance, and I mean huge. It was fat and went from floor to ceiling. I had to follow little colored footsteps to the reception desk. My mom and I were then taken into a back alcove where my vitals were taken. Next was a patient room where I waited for about five minutes, at which time a young woman pregnant with her first child walked in, and introduced herself as Katie, a genetic counselor. She took down my family history, and said the geneticist would be in shortly. My mom and I waited…and waited…and waited some more. About 45 minutes to an hour later, a young, vibrant lady walked in. "I am Dr. Shur the geneticist, and it is a pleasure to meet you! I am so excited to get to meet with a 34 year old who wants to discuss the possibility of having effects from fetal alcohol. I have never had a patient your age."

The geneticist began to study my face, my hands, and my now bare feet. She made notes on a piece of paper, and took out a diagnostic book. She would jot down some physical characteristics I had, and then refer to her book, explaining what she was writing and researching. "You definitely have a long, thin philtrum (the area between your nose and upper lip). You have slight palpebral fissures for both eyes, the left more so than the right (this is the distance between the corners of your eyes). You also have hockey stick formations on both palms (lines on my palms). Oh and yes, your pinky toes are characteristic as well (hypoplasia of the pinky toes, no toenails ever formed).

She took out a tape measure, and measured my head. "Your head size is in the 3rd to 10th percentile. This is so hard to diagnose, especially because I don't know what your head size should've been at birth. I did not have the opportunity to hear it from your birth mom's lips that she drank throughout her pregnancy. You say friends of hers said she drank every day. You say they told you she was drinking when she went into labor. Your adoptive mom was told she may have been drunk during the delivery. Looking at your infant photos, you had classic features of Fetal Alcohol Syndrome. Presently, at 34, I will say you definitely have effects of fetal alcohol. I would even say Fetal Alcohol Syndrome, but without getting the opportunity to speak to your birth mom, I can't write that as a diagnosis. I do believe you have it though. " She went on to say that had my birth mom not drank, there is a possibility I would not struggle with the concepts I do. "Your brain may have been different." I took it as, "I would've been smarter." She recommended I see a Behavioral Cognitive therapist, but was unable to refer me to one, because each one she made referrals to worked with children. At that moment, she stopped and looked at me and my mom. She told me I was a beautiful, successful woman, and told my mom that she had done an amazing job raising me. My mom's answer was, "We just treated her like a child, and gave her lots of love." The doctor's diagnosis was what I wanted to hear. That may sound odd, but it is the answer I needed for all the "whys" of the many impulsive choices I have made in life. This diagnosis explained so many of my "quirks". After my diagnosis was stated, the geneticist told my mom and me a story about one of her patients, and how the mother sobbed when her adopted child was given the diagnosis of Fetal Alcohol Syndrome. She told us that she was so happy to have met me, because she can now say she met a 34 year old who has had a successful life with Fetal Alcohol Syndrome. She was encouraged that I am a successful employee, daughter, wife and mother. Those words touched my core. As I was putting my coat on to leave the doctor's office, I turned to my mom and hugged her. I thanked her for attending with me. She returned the embrace, and said she was sorry I had struggled throughout my life because of fetal alcohol. I told her it was not her fault; her and my father did everything they could for me. I thanked her for raising me the way she did. I reiterated what the geneticist had stated, that I was as successful as I was because of the environment I was raised in.

We left the doctor's office and went to lunch. I was all revved up with positive energy, having a diagnosis and now a specialist who would be able to help me! A couple weeks after I received the diagnosis of Fetal Alcohol Syndrome, I followed the geneticist's advice, and obtained a Behavioral Cognitive Therapist to work with me on my impulsive behavior. The Behavioral Cognitive Therapist has me work through my impulsivity using a technique called *Mindfulness*. It is all about slowing down and thinking before you act. You have to think of each consequence there could be if you act on an impulse. It sounds simple, but it takes immense brain power to change the way your brain waves want to go. It is like changing the direction of a current in a pool. You have to use all of your muscles and really push forward to make a change.

Having a diagnosis has given me the ability to look back over the years of my life, and certain struggles and certain personality traits. I was finally able to explain so many "quirks."

I began to notice my impulsivity in my early 30s, but had no idea why I was like this. My husband and mother would ask me to explain my behaviors and all I could say was, "It's just me, I don't have an answer." I originally associated my impulsivity to being adopted in the sense that I thought I was just protecting myself from being hurt and feeling the pain I subconsciously may have felt when my birth mom gave me over to the nurses. By spewing out words or performing actions without thinking, I would do what I wanted before anybody could say or do anything. It turns out my impulsive behavior has nothing to do with being adopted, but does have to do with the choice my birth mother made to drink while pregnant with me. My impulsivity is not just when I speak. If you are familiar with the saying, "Actions speak louder than words," that is so true of some of my behaviors. My impulsivity transcends into behaviors, some of which have threatened my marriage and caused friction between my parents and I in high school. Decisions such as going to happy hours on Fridays with co-workers, and staying out until 3 in the morning. Not thinking my husband and children have not had much time with me all week, yet my coworkers see me all day, Monday through Friday. I never stopped to think. I just saw the words Happy Hour in my head, and knew I wanted to drink and chill. I was not being a responsible adult, wife or parent. Now I was able to link my behaviors to a reason. The reason did not negate my behavior, but it helped me understand myself and my brain.

For years now, my mom has had conversations with family and friends, and she has made the comment that throughout my childhood into young adulthood I never took an interest in activities she enjoyed. When she first mentioned this, I took offense to it. Then over time I started to think about that statement. It had validity. So, because I love to find out the whys of things, and love to investigate, I started wondering why that statement was true. I started to think about my friends and my family members. My friend Carol had grown up with her mom who stayed home with her four children. She was an amazing stay at home mom. Her mom used to have these birthday parties with all these neat little games. Carol grew up to have two boys, and she had a party for her oldest at her house, and had these neat little games for the children to play. I just thought about her mom, and how they were so alike in that manner. Carol's father is an engineer, and loves to work on household projects. Carol and her husband moved into a house, and Carol would talk to me on the phone about how she had spent the evening taping her walls in the dining room so her and her husband could paint the next day. She then went on to tell me she moved an electrical outlet and fixed the wiring. Those years growing up with her parents, she was watching and learning. Now she follows in their footsteps. My friend Melissa grew up with a stay at home mom who then went into the work force as her children got older. Her grandmother would come to her parents' house and clean the house. Everything was always in its place, always so tidy. Now that Melissa is married with two children, I see her mom's influence on her. She is a stay at home mom, but plans to enter the work force once her children are older. She keeps her house as tidy as her parents did. My sister in law is Italian, and she grew up with Pasta dinners on Sunday nights. Her mom used to make a huge spread. On Christmas Eve, her family used to follow the Seven Fishes tradition. When she got married to my husband's brother, she would do the Seven Fishes for Christmas Eve, just like her mother used to. She also tries to do Sunday pasta dinners like her mother used to, when time allows. I look at my husband. His grandfather was a chef, and he used to watch him make amazing desserts such as cheesecake. My husband cooks for our family and enjoys doing it. He loves to make meals where presentation is just as amazing as the taste. I look around at each of these people, and I realize they have followed in family footprints. I never did. My mom loved to shop for clothes. She always looked chic, she still does. I never liked to shop for clothes. I hated the mall. I used to dress in whatever was easy and comfortable (sweatpants and sweatshirts), I would always put my hair up in a ponytail. She loves to cook hearty, healthy meals. We always had an amazing home cooked meal when I was home. I never watched her cook meals. My mom also loved to work outside, pruning bushes and gardening. I never watched her as a little girl, never pretended to garden when I would play outside, and to this day have no interest in it. My father is a mechanical engineer who, like my friend Carol's father, loves to do household projects. I never watched him at length do projects or asked him how to start or finish projects. I have realized that I am a unique individual in that I did not follow in anyone's footsteps. I have sat with my husband and told him I don't do anything special for our family. I do laundry. That is it. I also consider myself a good mother. I guess one could say I inherited my mom and dad's love and adoration for children.

Now, my family and I are very close knit. We do many activities together that we all enjoy. We go Kayaking, we sit and tell stories about the past, we love to get coffee together and chat. I have always felt I belonged with the Kulaks, I have always felt like a Kulak, I have always been a Kulak. I used to be stumped as to why I never took an interest in some of the activities that my mother and father considered their hobbies. I thought, like many things, maybe my interests were related to being adopted. Maybe those traits my friends and their families have in common hold a genetic component, a component my parents and I do not share. Given my diagnosis of FAS, I now believe the alcohol in utero is the reason I never tried to learn to cook with my mom, or do household projects with my dad. FAS explains why I never concerned myself with gardening. It even explains why I didn't enjoy shopping and was content to dress in sweats with no makeup. Each of these events requires following directions which can be complex at times, and shopping has lots of bright colors, bright lights and many decisions to be made. This can all be overwhelming for a brain that has been affected by alcohol. I felt relief when I made these connections. It all made more sense to me than not being from the same gene pool as my family. So much more sense.

My mom and I have asked myself one question multiple times, and actually, until recently, never came up with an answer that made sense. "Why was I so distant from my first son, Dominic?" I thought it was me being a first time mom and overwhelmed. My mom and I both thought I was also subconsciously mourning how my birth mom gave me up at birth, and I had to sort through the feelings of abandonment. As I look back now with new knowledge, I think all of the previously stated definitely played a role, but the main player in the game was my birth mom's chronic alcoholism. Fetal Alcohol Syndrome affects the brain, and many with FAS have issues with behavior and intellect (www.nofas.org, 2014). Some struggle with brand new concepts, such as taking care of a child, where there is so much to know, more than one *right way,* and multitasking is a necessity. There are many things happening at once (the baby crying, needing a diaper change, changing a diaper and the baby pees and poops all over, and then he needs a bottle). There is so many different events happening simultaneously, it is sensory overload, which often affects those with FAS (www.nofas.org, 2014). I had my son at 28 years old, but

I am about 10 years immature, thanks to FAS. I had to mature a bit through learning to take care of my first born. I had an immense family support group, and within a couple months, I was on my way to being a well-adjusted, confident mom (as confident as a first time mom can be).

I think back to when I was in high school and had my driver's license. My friend and I enjoyed going out to dinner on the weekends. Bertuccis in Columbia Maryland was our favorite dining place. We would take turns driving. When it was my turn, these are the words my friend Melissa always heard. She could mouth the words before I said them: "Um, I don't remember which way I turn to get to the restaurant, Melissa." I *always* didn't remember. Keep in mind, I had driven to Bertuccis Restaurant about 6 times since having my license and still would get confused. I always thought it was just who I was. I thought it was a "girl" thing. I didn't know later on in life I would actually be able to trace it back to being addicted to alcohol before I was born.

FAS also effects my ability to understand abstract concepts. Now I understand why word problems were my nemesis throughout my elementary school years. Well, at least I tried to learn them. After many attempts, and assistance from my dad, I would get the right answer. I would get one problem finally correct, writing the correct answer on a torn and eraser stained piece of paper. I would look at the next word problem and my eyes would become blurry with tears of frustration. The only difference would be one problem would use apples and the next would use oranges, but that one word confused me. I became lost.

"Oh Rebecca, that is such a nice card! Thank you so much!" My mother in law remarked one time on her birthday. "Now, Dominic signed the card for all of you?" I remember looking at her, and laughing. "Nope, that would be my handwriting." My son was 5 at the time, I was 33. I remember in elementary school our grades In Maryland were always *1-5*, *1* being amazing, *5* being poor. I always, *always* got a *2* in handwriting. My handwriting never improved from third grade on. I just assumed it was because I was left handed. That is not the case. My birth mom indirectly had a part in my handwriting ability. Her drinking affected my fine motor skills.

After my diagnosis, my attitude wavered between excitement, relief at having a reason for my "quirks", and anger. Anger at my birth mom. Anger because I have talked to people she worked with, people she considered her family and friends. They all said she drank throughout her entire pregnancy with me, and denied knowing she was pregnant. Her one co-worker and friend told me everyone thinks Joanie knew she was pregnant but chose to bury her head in the sand. I could've not struggled in school, maybe

I wouldn't have made the poor decisions I did. In the end though, it is what it is. I am a successful woman who now has answers to why I do certain things the way I do. I decided that I can't change the past, but I can change the future, and I will. I learned after my meeting with the geneticist that if my tears of realization can be someone else's tears of hope, then I have made a positive impact on a small part of society. I don't know what the future holds for me but I am more than ready to walk through those doors that await me.

Chapter Nineteen

My Voice on Adoption

When I met my husband Jason back in 2000, and we were getting to know one another, of course we discussed our views on children. We both agreed one day we would love to have children. I opened my heart to him, and divulged that I thought I may want to adopt a baby. I wanted to give back. My husband listened to me, and by the sincere look in his eyes and serious look on his face, I knew he understood. Jason and I got married, and we still maintained that we wanted to hear the pitter patter of little

feet, but we made sure we established our lives first. Once

we had stable jobs and a house, we discussed having

children. Four years passed after our wedding day, and

Dominic Matthew was born. He was, and still is the light

of both of our lives. Four years following Dominic's birth,

Nicolas Richard was born. Another constant beacon of

light in our lives. We had discussed throughout our

marriage about wanting to adopt a child, but so far we have

not walked down that road. It is not because our views on

adoption have changed since we first met. We both believe

it is an amazing life changing event for both adopted

parents and adoptees. At the present moment in our life,

adoption is not in the forefront. We would love to help a

child have a stable life and grow to be a strong individual.

We both know if we chose adoption at this point in our

life, we would not be able to support that child the way

they deserve to be supported. It would not be fair to that

child. Children who are placed for adoption deserve the best chance at life they can be given. Their adoptive parents should do their best to be their compass so they can see the world, and become who they want to be. My parents were my compass throughout my younger years, and I still look to them to guide me through muddy waters. They have ingrained in me to believe in myself and follow my dreams. I do go off course at times, but my parents have taught me mistakes are a part of life, and perseverance will prevail. I have taken their lessons with me as I have matured, and have become a strong, independent woman.

 I hope that if one day, adoption crosses my husband's and my path, I will instill in our adoptive children the invaluable lessons my parents taught me.

I believe adoption is a learning process for all involved. For the adoptive parents, there are lessons to be learned about accepting a child that does not share your genetics as your own. There are lessons about opening one's eyes to the inner struggles the adopted child may face, and understanding that both adoptees and adoptive parents may need to be educated on how to deal with these struggles. Adoption is a learning process for the adoptee as they struggle to figure out where they belong in life and who they are. It is also a learning process for the adoptive parents on how to deal with their own emotions and those of their adopted child. It can be a process to decide to search for your biological roots, or maybe not to search, because you feel complete already. Adoption is a myriad of emotions and processes, with multiple pathways to be discovered.

Chapter Twenty

Hindsight

One constant about everyone's life is that there is always a multitude of events that make up who we are. It is never just one thing that defines us. Throughout my journey, I have realized that it is not just feelings of being an adoptee that define who I am and my "quirks," but also having Fetal Alcohol Syndrome. Although mild, this disorder defines and explains so many characteristics I originally thought were due to being an adoptee. I think both events join together to make me who I am. It isn't clearly one or the other, but a blend.

As I looked back over my search and reunion, I started to dissect my methods. I started to ask myself, what would I change, what would I keep and what do I want other adoptees to take away from this search? I decided to take myself back to the beginning, the very first day I sat down at my computer and decided I wanted to find Joan. The internet is an amazing tool. Just by typing in a first name and a state, it produces pages of websites for review. I have to say, doing it this way is extremely overwhelming, and I started to think everyone and anyone could be my birth mom. If you are a person who knows your limits and knows when to take breaks so as not to become consumed, then typing in a couple words from your non-identifying sheet may be a good start for you. If you are similar to me, in that you are forever an optimist and always see what you think is your answer but in fact is so far from the answer, then you may need to seek out research assistance. There are resources out there that I had never even heard about. I perused all the adoption registries I could find. I came across www.adopeeconnect.com (Adoptee Connect.com, 2004), and within this registry was the link to the ALMA society (Adoptees Liberty Movement Association). I took the list of Joans born 8/11/1940 that the ALMA society had given me, and began my own investigation, making sure to email a worker named Candy when I had crossed off names so she could cross them off on her end as well. There were a couple people who helped me sort through the list, but I was the one who pushed through every day, using the internet any way I could to cross out or keep names.

Candy was one person at ALMA who stayed connected with me until I had every name crossed off. She was patient with me and she read my crazed emails that had all of my hypothetical questions about the list of names. I had mentioned The ALMA society requested a money order.

They are a Non-Profit organization, and the upkeep of the organization depends on donations and registration fees. I strongly encourage adoptees who are searching to join this society. The amount of money they request isn't extraordinary, and being part of a group that understands what an adoptee is going through, and supporting you in your quest for truth, well I don't think you can put a price on that.

Another registry I joined was the ISRR (International Soundex Reunion Registry). They are also non for profit, and request a nominal fee to join. The Alma Society strongly encouraged me to get into this registry, as they use Soundex, which is a code which was used in the American Census in 1880 and after. What's unique about Soundex is that it matches up names based on how names sound, not on spelling. More matches to names are made this way. This is another registry I would encourage adoptees to join.

Of course, I entered multiple other adoption registries online. I googled Adoption registries, and New Jersey adoption registries. Any I could join, I did. All of the online registries I joined cost nothing to join. None of the registries came up with any matches, and that is only because Joan had been dead since 1999. What is imperative when joining registries, if you find who you are searching for, please go back to every registry and update it stating a match has been made. The registries ask that you do this so nobody goes into the registry, including biological relatives who may be searching for you, and you have already solved your puzzle.

Another tip from one adoptee to another is when you begin searching, get yourself a binder with folders. I had this fake leather zipper up folder with pockets everywhere. I kept a sheet with every registry I joined, and I kept every correspondence I had with everyone associated to my adoption and my search. I also had a folder in my email titled, *JOAN.* All email correspondence went into this email folder. After a couple months, as I started receiving emails from the social worker and emails from search angels and then emails from Joan's friends, I had to subdivide the folder into multiple folders, one for each category of people I met along my journey. Order is a necessity when searching. It helps to keep the search organized, because your brain can be severely scattered with emotions and what ifs throughout the process.

Search Angels are another part of my journey that I strongly recommend. They are indeed angels. There were two angels that were there every step of the way through my journey. The first one I started speaking to was Diana. It turned out she was also born and raised in Northern New Jersey. I believe fate brought her to me, and she worked night and day to try to solve the Joan case. She, like Candy, read my crazy emails with my happy, sad and confused emotions within the written text. She would always respond, and always had a way with words.

Usually search angels are connected with adoption in some way. Diana's spouse Steph is an adoptee, and Diana was able to really empathize with the emotions I was going through. I remember there was a time when I was feeling pretty low about finding Joan. I was so frustrated at the state of New Jersey, at their sealed adoption records, at the fact the social worker knew her last name and could not disclose it. I wanted to continue to search, but I also wanted to give up. Two emotions exact opposite of one another, but I felt both at the same time. This journey had many times where opposite emotions were felt simultaneously. I remember I spilled into an email these feelings to Diana. She wrote me back that Steph would speak to me over the phone about my emotions, if I felt like talking to someone. She then revealed that Steph never offered this as an option for her friends. I felt blessed. I never ended up making that phone call. Instead I took a step back from my search, and I just let every emotion fill my soul. The emotions shuddered through me like a chill, one right after another. Anger, sadness, frustration, boom, boom, boom. Afterward, I felt clear headed again. I knew Steph was there if I needed her, and for that I was thankful. Diana was amazing because she loved to search for lost family members, but she also had a good sense of humor. It was her humor and her gentle spirit that kept me going so many nights. If she hadn't decided to try Classmates.com, I may not know who Joan Chanowski is. I decided to give it a shot because Diana had tried it, and although the Joans she found were not my birth mother, it gave me the most hope I had felt through the entire search. Diana and I still keep in touch, and she still makes me laugh.

Elaine is the other search angel I met. I actually met her through an extremely strong woman I met on Sherrie Eldridge's Yahoo Adoptee Group. Elaine had helped her through some tough searching times, and she gave me her information. Elaine turned out to be from Maryland, and lived in a town about 25 minutes from where I had lived from birth until I was 18 years old. I know fate played a role in us crossing each other's paths as well. Elaine is a birth mother who reunited with her son. She also read my rambling emails and was patient with the search when I was not. Elaine is the person who relayed to me that Joan had died. She was hopeful she was incorrect, and the information was about someone else. She did not just email me the information that my birth mom was dead. She called me. She was an amazing support. We didn't speak long on the phone. She knew I needed to digest the information. Elaine and I still keep in touch, and I am so thankful she stood by me the entire way.

I want to let adoptees know that I think it is important to have a couple people who can somehow relate to your situation of being adopted in your support circle. If you do not know anyone personally, a support group for adoptees, either online or an actual group you attend can be extremely beneficial. I was fortunate in that my best friend Stacey is an adoptee. We both attended undergraduate school together and were in the same major. We never really hung out until after we graduated and started attending the same graduate school. I remember parking my car in a parking lot to go to a graduate class, and Stacey pulled into the same lot. We walked to class together, and somehow we got on the topic of her being adopted. I remember thinking that was so cool, because now I had a friend who could relate to me. Stacey was also adopted at birth, and has similar questions about who her birth mother is, if she has any siblings, and who her birth father is. Stacey is the one friend I can speak to about being adopted, and she gets it. She didn't sit across from me and tell me she did not understand why I have an amazing family yet still yearned to know who Joan was. She has been there for me throughout this search journey, and she is an incredibly strong woman. She found out when she was twenty four that she has a health issue that nobody knows if genetics play a part in or not. This is another reason adoptees records should not be sealed. Her medical history could answer so many questions for her. Stacey came into my life for a reason, she came into my life to be my best friend, a lifelong support for searching for ones roots, and to teach me that having a positive outlook on life really does make your life one full of blessings and promise.

There is one other woman I met when I first started my journey to finding Joan. Her name is Ann, and I met her through Sherrie Eldridge's Yahoo Adoptee Group discussion site. She is the woman who put me in touch with Elaine. Ann is a strong, beautiful individual, who I connected with emotionally. We are both adoptees, and she is another adoptee who has been through a life event where family medical history was pertinent, but was not to be found. She looked to her family for medical history for her child, and was told by a family member it didn't matter, she and her brother had been adopted at birth. Ann was in her 40s when she first learned she was adopted. Her adoptive parents had since passed, so she was unable to find out the reason why she was never told. Ann showed immense courage, perseverance and strength in the journey she has been through. I have been able to speak openly and freely with her without fear of being judged about my feelings about being adopted and wanting to search for my roots. Ann has always been there to listen and to give advice. The emotional roller coaster I was on she could relate to, and she would email me words of encouragement. She is a woman who crossed into my adoption path for many reasons, and for that I will be forever grateful.

As I sat back and thought about all of the events that occurred throughout my search, I tried to think about what events I would've gone about in a different way. The first event that crossed my mind was how I would get phone numbers and just call people, asking if they were my birth mother or if they knew of her. In the back of my mind, I knew I was being selfish. On the other end of that phone could've been my birth mother. I wanted answers, and I didn't stop to think of the effect it could have on Joan if she had answered the phone. The funny thing is, I would talk to my family and friends about my search method, and how I had to be careful and think about Joan's feelings. I think I believed if I talked about how I should feel, it would make up for the fact that I never practiced what I preached. I think sending letters to prospective birth mothers is alright to do. It could have a similar effect as a phone call, but at least with a letter the birth mother is not put on the spot to respond right away. With a letter she has time to gather her thoughts and decide what she would like the future to hold.

The next part of my search and reunion journey I would've changed is being more aware of my ability to become so consumed in the search. When I started out searching, I told myself I would do it once the children went to bed. I told myself I would limit it to three nights per week, and then only up to one hour on those nights. Well, I stuck to the schedule probably 60 % of the time. I didn't think that was too horrible. Except I let moments with my family go, and you can't ever get those back. I realize I have a right to search for my past but it is all about balance. I left out a core part of my balancing act though. My husband. I would put the children to bed and then surf the internet until I went to bed. I rarely considered how my husband may be feeling during my searches. Even if I caught a glimpse that he may want to spend time with me, and I sat down to watch a movie with him, I would have my phone glued to my hand, and I would be searching throughout our "date night." My advice for those adoptees who have families or friends who enjoy hanging out with you, make a calendar for yourself, or a chart. Just like you would do for all of your appointments you may have with doctors and teachers and dentists. Sketch out time for your search, and then go over it with your family and friends. Make sure they are ok with the schedule and that they do not feel left out and ignored. I didn't do that. I figured I could juggle everyone without asking them how they felt about it. I was selfish in my searching. It is very easy to become consumed, like I explained in an earlier chapter. I think making your search time visual, and discussing your action plan with those you love may be a good way to find a balance.

Another piece of advice I would like to give to adoptees concerns how to proceed after finding your birth family. When I found Mark and his family, they immediately held their arms open to me. I made a decision within four months that I was going to meet them. Looking back, that was a rather quick decision. I am not one to dwell on whether or not to do something. If I want to do something, I do it. I don't consider the consequences like I should. I let those I love do that for me. Then when my friends and family tell me their concerns, I get angry, defensive, and shut down, and do what I want anyway. My advice is to try your best as an adoptee to keep your ears and heart open. I understand how exciting and life altering it is to find genes that fit you, finally, after so many months or years of searching. I understand how when you finally find your biological relatives, some of you may want to make plans to meet them right away, as to not let them slip through your hands like they slipped through the past years of your life. It is always easier to give advice standing from the outside looking in. I also think the advice given from the outside looking in usually has merit. Of course, I am writing this now, but when I had just found my biological uncle and my cousins, I didn't want to hear any negative talk about travelling to Texas. Everyone who gave me advice was not giving me advice because they disagreed with my desire to go and meet my birth family. I did see it that way though at first, I will be honest. They were giving me advice because they loved and cared about me and did not want me to get hurt. Nobody knew my birth family. They turned out to be wonderful fun people, but what if they turned out to be crazy people? You can't stop your life and decide you are not going to take any risks because of the possible negative outcomes. All you can do is listen to the people that care about you. Even if you decide against their advice, at least listen to the advice and consider it. You are your own person, but this is a big decision. It never hurts to have more than your own opinion when it comes to big decisions. I decided I was flying out to Texas to meet my birth family, and even when I sat down with my husband and we both agreed the money was just not there, I left that conversation saying to myself, ok let's find good flight deals now. I am the type of person who will say what someone else wants to hear, even though my own agenda is the exact opposite. I always want to please people while making sure I get what I want also. I found cheap flights, and then told my husband I really wanted to go to Texas, and I would be fine on my own. A better way to go about that whole scenario would have been to sit down with my husband before I found the cheap flights and tell him of my plan. Tell him that although I knew money was tight, and he was not fond of me going by myself to meet people we didn't know, that was my plan. I should've made him aware that I knew of his fears, but it was something I felt I really needed to do. Just try to keep in mind that the people that are concerned for you are concerned because they don't want you to be disappointed or to get hurt.

The next piece of advice I want to give adoptees involves who to take with you when you go to meet your

biological family. It is a personal decision. Every person
is different, every person has different comfort levels.
Some need lots of support from familiar faces, while some
prefer to connect with their roots on their own.

When I decided I was going to fly to Texas to meet
my biological family, I had multiple conversations with my
friends and family about whether I should go alone or with
family. I was torn. A big part of me wanted to go by
myself. I was going to be worried enough about the
Chrzanowski's impression of me, I didn't want to worry
about their impression of my husband as well. My decision
was made pretty easy in the beginning because my husband
and I couldn't afford both of us to take flights. I had
purchased my ticket, but as the time drew closer, I had
conversations with my sister in law Francesca and my in-
laws. I also spoke to fellow adoptees on the Yahoo site on
the subject. They all were apprehensive about me going
alone. Adoptees who had been in my situation told me to

take someone. I took their words under careful consideration, being that they had been where I was standing. My in-laws offered to pay my husband's way to Texas, so I would not have to go alone. My husband chose to not go, due to us having two children and him having to work. Being the people pleaser that I am, I lost sleep at night worrying how upset my whole family would be if I chose to go alone. Throughout the time I chose to go to the time the plane departed, my parents were the only ones that understood I needed to go alone. They told me they would be there for support, and my father offered to come with me, if I thought I did want someone to go, and finances were an issue. I thought about my father's offer over a few days, off and on. First I thought it would be awesome, because my dad would get to meet Joan's family. Then in the next breath I thought it would be very awkward. So, my final decision was to go by myself. It was the right decision for me. Please remember, this is a personal decision, and every situation is different. I just want to let adoptees know to weigh all the options, and choose the one that is best for them. Others may not agree with your decision, but in the end you need to walk away from that first encounter feeling you made the right choice.

When I made the final decision to travel to Texas alone, I had another decision to make. Where would I stay? When I originally told J I was going, I told him I would definitely stay in a hotel. Then I did what I always do, I guess I could call it a "Rebeccaism." I told J that Mark and his wife were insistent I stay with them. I told J this, but told him that I was not comfortable staying with them. I went ahead and booked a hotel. I called Mark and told him where my reservations were. He was not having it. He did not want me at a hotel in a city I was unfamiliar with. So, I cancelled the hotel. I continued to look for a hotel closer to Mark's house. I told Mark I was going to stay in a hotel because I needed my down time and I liked my own bathroom. Mark, being a marine was very persuasive and persistent. I ended up folding to the words of a man I had never met. I told my husband I was going to stay with Mark and his wife. My husband, in addition to everyone else, tried to talk me out of it. They all had the same words of advice: They were sure Mark and Nancy were wonderful people, but everyone, including my fellow adoptees online said I was going to need a place to have down time. I agreed with that statement. I told everyone I would look for a hotel…once again. Well, I did search for a hotel, but I never booked one. The night before I left, my husband asked me to leave the hotel information where I was going to be staying. My stomach turned. I had not had the final conversation with J telling him the hotel was Hotel Chrzanowski. The morning came, and J drove me to Newark Airport in New Jersey. He dropped me off, we said our goodbyes, and I entered the airport, ready to embark on a life altering journey. When I got into the terminal, and I was waiting for my flight, I emailed J and wrote that I would be staying with Mark. I knew I was in trouble. I had lied to my husband. Why? I had done it because I knew he would not approve of my decision. Even though at one point when I had told him I was staying with them, he had said it was my journey and my decision. I guess I didn't want to hear the tone of disapproval. My parents approved of my staying with Mark and Nancy. My mom said it made her feel more at ease knowing I was not in some hotel in a state I had never been, all by myself. So, at least the little girl in me was happy. I had my parents' approval. Yet, the approval that should've mattered is J's. Nobody else's. He was my husband, my partner, my main emotional support through this entire journey. He would forgive me in time, but it was not worth lying to him at all. I lied to him to make my biological uncle happy, a man I had yet to meet. My advice to adoptees is this: If you are given the opportunity to meet your biological family, and they are states away, or it will involve travelling and staying more than one day, be open and honest about your intentions with your significant other and those that care about you. In the end, yes your choice is yours to make, and yours alone, but do not complicate matters and emotions any more than they may already be.

I want to let those searching know that the excitement and anticipation you will feel searching and finding your biological roots may only be one sided. I am sharing this, because nobody told me. I wish someone had. I found out through the few years I have known my birth family, as the phone calls and the texts have become less frequent. I had started to think like they didn't want anything to do with me, that I was just a nuisance. My husband and I had chats about these feelings I had, and he put it into perspective for me.

Joan was not a part of her family's lives after 1963. They grew up with their families and friends, made their lives and are living them. I too have grown up with my family and friends, made my life and am living it. The difference is, I had anticipation from the moment I started searching for my birth mom. I had anticipation of not only finding Joan, but the rest of her family as well. That anticipation was one sided. They didn't know I ever existed, until I reached out to them.

My biological family does not dislike me. They like me. They enjoyed my visit with them in 2013. They just were never searching for me, so they had no preconceived notions and hopes of finding me. I made the decision to let them go on with their lives, and if they reach out on occasion, that is wonderful. If they do not, then I have memories, and wonderful ones at that. I have found my history, and I will never forget them. It was a very hard lesson for me to come to terms with. It hurts, and it is difficult to not take it personally. I am working towards that everyday though. I know they love me as a friend. I have chosen to move forward as they have.

The last piece of advice I would like to offer to adoptees is when you are searching for your beginning, make an effort to at times stop everything you are doing, and just sit. Open your heart, your mind and your soul to feeling. Throughout my journey of searching, so many emotions surfaced, and I never was prepared for them. Going into my search, I thought I would just handle the emotions like I do every day. Spend five minutes on them and move forward. I thought I would never let my emotions show in front of people and never let them hear fear or sadness in my voice. That is how I have gone through life, and my search was no different. When I met Joan's family, every day was go go go. When my head hit the pillow at night, I fell asleep immediately. I never made time to decompress and to take in everything that had taken place. An adoptees search journey can be long, slow and complicated or it can be quick, easy and fun. It can be all of these things. It can be so much more, and so much less. Each journey is unique. If you do get to reunite with your biological family, please make sure you allow yourself down time. I thought my emotions would be quick to process, but every day, months after my reunion, I find myself going back to Texas, back to my first encounter with everyone. I become choked up, I find myself having feelings of immense happiness, immense bewilderment, and immense sadness for the reunion that had everyone but Joan. I expect those feelings to come and go for the rest of my days, but not with quite the intensity that they currently are. If I had taken the time to myself to take the experience in, a little time every day, every night as I was going through the reunion, I think the feelings would not be as intoxicating all at once. The feelings aren't negative ones by any means, but maybe they would be less distracting throughout my days if I had taken time to feel the emotions while I was going through them.

I think adoptees should try to express their feelings throughout their search journey in a way that works for them. I chose to discuss my journey on the Yahoo Adoptee site Sherrie Eldridge has (Jewel Among Jewels Adoption Network, Inc, 2013). I also wrote poetry, and eventually blogged for Adoption.com (Elevati.com, 2014). Writing is my release, it always has been. Writing is not everyone's way to express their emotions. Some may like to discuss their emotions with someone they know, or with a counselor. Whatever your outlet may be, I think it is very important to utilize it throughout your search. Like I mentioned earlier, the emotional path can have an array of emotions. They can become overwhelming. If you do not know what your outlet is, talk to other adoptees to find out if they have an outlet, and try it out to see if it is helpful for you. Maybe talk to a counselor for ideas. The search process can be frustrating and disheartening and exciting; within hours the mood can change. Having an outlet can be healthy, and can help you deal with the emotional turmoil that can occur.

Receiving a diagnosis of Fetal Alcohol Syndrome as an adult answered so many questions about the past 34 years. I was relieved. I am hopeful that I can give hope to those parents who have children affected by FAS, and give them insight that a strong, supportive environment to grow up in, one with routine, usually makes for a successful life. I am yearning to get my story out to obstetricians, health clinics, neuropsychologists, and primary care physicians so a movement can begin to educate these specialists in knowing and understanding the signs and symptoms of FAS. Not in just children, but also in adults.

I went into my own search thinking I would discover Joan Chanowski in a couple months. I never expected the twists, turns, divots or uphills my search turned into. Through talking to other adoptees online, I was given websites to try and people to contact. Everyone that I came into contact with turned into another lead, and eventually, I found my birth mom and my birth family. I expected while I was still searching that Joan may have passed away. I never expected to end up with her ashes in my cedar closet. My entire search was intertwined with fate. Joan's ashes ending up in her biological daughter's hands was an act of fate. I am aware not everyone believes in fate or acts of a higher power. However you want to look at my journey, fate or not, it was a journey of discovery, of learning, of family lost and family found. It was an incredible journey that ended with a girl finding her birth mom, a birth mother finally getting the peace she deserved, and a girl and a family finding each other and having their hearts woven together with ribbons of heredity and love.

About the Author

Rebecca Tillou grew up in Ellicott City, Maryland with her parents and older brother. She attended The State University of New York College at Geneseo, and graduated with a Bachelor's Degree in Communicative Sciences and Disorders, aka Speech Pathology. She worked with preschoolers as a speech therapist after college for about 3 years, and now works as a claim specialist at an insurance company. She also is a storyteller for adoption.com. She is married to a wonderful, supportive husband and has two beautiful, healthy little boys. She currently resides in Voorheesville, NY, and continues to campaign for the FASD community and the adoption community through doing presentations at conferences and colleges. She can be reached at rltillou25@gmail.com.

Her book is also on Amazon Kindle.

She thanks you for joining her in her journey.